MALCOLM HILLIER'S
COLOUR GARDEN

MALCOLM HILLIER'S
COLOUR GARDEN

Photography by
STEPHEN HAYWARD AND STEVEN WOOSTER

BCA
LONDON NEW YORK SYDNEY TORONTO

A DORLING KINDERSLEY BOOK

PROJECT EDITOR Gillian Roberts
ART EDITOR Deborah Myatt
MANAGING EDITOR Mary-Clare Jerram
MANAGING ART EDITOR Amanda Lunn
PRODUCTION Meryl Silbert

This edition published 1996 by BCA
by arrangement with Dorling Kindersley Limited
CN 5135

First published in Great Britain in 1995
by Dorling Kindersley Limited
9 Henrietta Street, London WC2E 8PS

Computer page make-up by Mark Bracey and
Deborah Myatt, Dorling Kindersley, Great Britain

Text film output by The Right Type, Great Britain

Reproduced by grb EDITRICE, Italy

Printed and bound in Great Britain by Butler & Tanner Ltd, Frome and London

CONTENTS

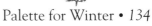

Colour

❖

How colour works to give different
effects has an endless fascination for
people interested in creating beautiful
surroundings. Like all abstract ideas,
colour theory is easier to understand
if it is placed in a familiar context.

COLOUR WHEEL

Throughout our waking hours, we live in a world of colour. Indoors and out, colour constantly excites our senses. It is hardly surprising, then, that colour affects not just our view of life but also our moods and feelings. And yet we don't often give much thought to colour: it's so familiar that for the most part we simply take it for granted. Lucky we gardeners! who are, I believe, more aware of colour than most people. How easily we conjure in our mind's eye an evergreen glade or the hue of a favourite rose. Even so, to understand a little more about using colour to create moods in the garden, we need a rainbow of our own and our own way of viewing it.

THE PRIMARIES

The three primary colours are red, blue, and yellow, arranged at right into a triangle. They are not made by mixing other colours: each one has its particular attributes. We're apt to see red as hot and rich; blue as cool and distant; and yellow as luminous and fresh. While red and yellow abound in the gardener's wheel, blue is not nearly as plentiful (if viewed in relative terms). This natural order of things is just as well, for red, yellow, and blue mixed in equal amounts together make a dark grey of the dullest hue.

THE SECONDARIES

The colours that are the secondaries are named green, orange, violet. These do not exist in their own right, as do the primaries, but are created by mixing pairs of the primary colours in equal amounts. Thus, green is made up from yellow and blue; orange from red and yellow; violet from red and blue. You can see the secondary colours in the picture as three individual triangles arranged around the inner primary triangle: each one spans the pair of primary colours from which it is made. Of the secondaries, green is for us the most important, for it is invariably present in the garden as foliage.

THE TERTIARIES

The primary and secondary colours are placed in the outer ring (*left*, in shadow) where the apex of each of their single triangles touches it. In the space that is left between each of them, you can make the tertiary colours by mixing each closest pair of primary and secondary colours. Thus – red and violet make purple; blue and violet create indigo; blue and green create turquoise; yellow and green make chartreuse; yellow and orange make gold; and red and orange make scarlet. These are all found in the rich world of plants except for blue-green turquoise, which is not a garden colour. But, in contrast to the primary and secondary colours, they are much harder to define: no two people will imagine them as exactly the same colours.

PROPERTIES OF YELLOW

❖

Primary yellow is the most joyous colour of the spectrum, shining from the warm part of the colour wheel as its brightest star. Being close to white, which is pure light, yellow has great clarity; and it's a forward colour, one to which the eye is quickly drawn. Seen with its immediate neighbours lime-green and gold, a warm harmony appears encompassing apricot and yolk-yellow beside rich luminous greens.

IN LYRICAL MOOD
A melodious mix of yellows, golds, gold-greens, and cream will bring beams of sunlight in endless succession to the garden. Soft yellow lupin spires beckon invitingly toward golden-leaved elder behind. Rose 'Golden Wings', cream sisyrinchium, and a foam of lime-green lady's mantle in front make the picture complete.

PALER SHADES

In the upper reaches of yellow are lemon, primrose, apricot. These are the pale renderings of the gold-green, true yellow, and gold that are seen here in the band below. Lying close to white, they are serene colours suffused with energy and clear light, the freshest of hues. All are well represented in flowers at every season – even (if on a smaller scale) in winter – and add a translucent brilliance to variegated foliage year-round.

TRUE COLOURS

Yellow fulfils the central role here, with golden green on its cooler left-hand side and gold to the warmer right. Gold and yellow are vital features of the garden, particularly in spring; through summer, and autumn too, they bring a vivid, bright cheerfulness to the landscape. Golden green is found mainly in foliage, borne on trees and shrubs such as beech, choisya, elaeagnus, and euonymus.

DARKER SHADES

In the lower reaches of yellow are mustard-yellow flanked by emerald green to the left with deep yolk-yellow to the right. These darker shades of yellow and its neighbours seen in the central band absorb light and reflect their colours in foliage and flowers, although mustard is least represented. Green is a constant in every tone of leaf, while yolk-yellow appears in a host of autumnal foliage tints.

PROPERTIES OF ORANGE

❖

Orange spells excitement, dynamism, and drama, but it's a colour that looks in two directions. On the downside, it subdues some colours. Purples and darker blues suffer under the influence of orange, which has the effect of dulling them, producing an overwhelming drab effect. Pure oranges are warm and gay, at their most vibrant set off against the contrast of pale blues, pinks, and incisive lime-greens.

FADING GLORY
The colour of amber reflects the sun as it dips lower toward the autumnal equinox. During early summer, hawthorn Crataegus prunifolia is wreathed in white flowers. Clusters of bright fruit follow in hues that combine wonderfully with the burned orange of the turning leaves. Many crabapples produce a similar effect.

PALER SHADES

Corn, apricot, and peach are the pastel variants of the true orange that sits at the heart of the square. With these shades, what may be thought of as the negative aspect of orange – its dulling effect – can be used to create beautiful muted moods. Combined with grey, old rose, or steely blue, they form vistas of soothing calm. For summer, roses, particularly hybrid teas, are plentiful in this range, and autumn has chrysanthemums.

TRUE COLOURS

Pure orange, at the centre of this band, has gold to the left: to the right is amber. Like all the colours related to orange, these conjure autumn at first glance, though of course there are many flowers in this range for summer and spring as well. Reinforced by the two colours at either side, orange presents a sunny and welcoming mood here – its most positive face.

DARKER SHADES

The deeper relatives of orange reveal another mood. In rust, burned orange, and blood-red the temperature climbs from comfortably warm to hot, and the pace quickens. These rich and powerful tones work best with the yellows and reds that juxtapose them on the colour wheel. They are made sombre in mixes with purple and dark blues, while white serves only to heighten their withdrawal.

PROPERTIES OF RED

❖

Primary red is a wonderful and, at the same time, difficult colour to use in the garden. Because it opposes green in the colour wheel, and because most gardens are full of greenery in the form of foliage, red tends to be almost too vibrant and exciting for comfort. There's little feeling of serenity around red: rather it's a blunt jab in the ribs; no sitting at ease here, but an insistent invitation to "up and at 'em".

BOMBARDED BY COLOUR

There are few flowers that have such a strong colour as these tulips flowering in spring – a season devoted not only to pastel hues. Their brilliant red and the speckled leaves that match the green-lichened bark make a startling combination. The velvety petal texture strengthens their colour so it jumps out even more.

PALER SHADES

Moving round from the warm side of the colour wheel into regions of cooler tones, pink combines here with peach to its left and mauve to its right in an odd but interesting way. These pale hues deliver a less demanding style of red. They mix with silver or gold foliage to conjure a mood that has an old-fashioned feel, one that is tranquil, with a slightly dusty air, yet still worthy of interest.

TRUE COLOURS

Here is pure red in the centre position, separating scarlet to the left side and purple to the right in a range of colour that can easily jar on one's eye and grate on one's sensibilities. It's particularly the outer two that fight with each other and give rise to feelings of turmoil and chaos. Disturbing mixes mean excitement too, so do not rule them out simply because they seem at odds with each other.

DARKER SHADES

The deep tones closely related to red are easier to respond to than those in the band above. Looking from far left to right, here are dusky dark maroon, a shade of blood-red that verges on black (found in many roses and dahlias), and a wonderful deep purple: all have an inner luminous warmth. These are colours that can be combined with red to make comfortable alliances, creating schemes of rich and glowing intensity.

PROPERTIES OF VIOLET

❖

Violet takes its cue from the flower of the same name. Like the shy sweet violet, it rarely reveals a showy face unless paired with the opposing contrast of bright yellow, which gets it jumping! Violet is at the dark, moody end of the colour range, as are its neighbours purple and, in particular, indigo. It's effective with blue-pink, silver, and grey, but dulls red, orange, and blue and looks muddy with them.

RETIRING ELOQUENCE
A gentle coloration of lilac flushed lavender puts pansy Viola x wittrockiana *at the pale extremity of violet. Set among allium flower capsules just about to open, and the juicy green of stems and leaves, it makes a summer planting of incredible simplicity.*

PALER SHADES

Three pale associates of violet appear in this top band. Blue-pink, taking centre place, has lilac-blue to its left-hand side and ice-pink to its right. The marvellous soft subtle quality of these colours works best in combination with plants that have silver or grey leaves. For flowers, perennials and shrubs such as lobelia and hydrangea give all of these shades, while myriad roses grace the garden with both blue- and ice-pink.

TRUE COLOURS

A soft shade of pure violet lies at the heart of the square and its middle band; to its left and right are indigo and raspberry-pink. While all three together form a companionable group, neither indigo nor pink make genial partners with violet on its own. A pale lemony cream introduces vitality to this mix and avoids a dispirited effect.

DARKER SHADES

The square is completed with deep violet at its core, flanked to the left by dark blue-purple and with fuchsia-pink lying to its right. These regal tones of the violet range (each with a rich depth of its own) receive an extra boost when the three combine. Aconitums (lovely, if poisonous), geraniums, and french lavender; delphiniums, roses, clematis: all offer superb choice in these vigorous hues.

PROPERTIES OF BLUE

❖

In the world of flowers, blue is a colour that excites wonder and frustration. Blue is cool, calm – and distant too. It's the most beautiful of colours, yet also the most elusive. Plenty of plants described as blue betray touches of red in rogue shades of lilac and mauve. True blues worth a search for their serene beauty include blue poppy *Meconopsis betonicifolia*, plumbago, veronicas, borage, and many delphiniums.

CELESTIAL VIEW

In certain lights, with the sun high aloft and filtered through pale green leaves, bluebells can appear incredibly blue. But when the sun is lower and the light warmer, less penetratingly bright, they can assume a mauvish hue. Whatever colour, these naturalized bluebells make a sight whose loveliness takes your breath away.

PALER SHADES

Seen in the topmost row from far left to right, lilac, ice-blue, and pale turquoise compose a soft trio in the pale reaches of blue. These gentle renderings of a colour that is annoyingly difficult to come by in its pure form give breathtaking mixes with true blue if green-tinged turquoise is the keynote. Still lovely (if a little less amazing) are plantings where lilac and other pinkish blues combine with blue and a bit of cream.

TRUE COLOURS

At the centre, true blue reigns supreme. To the left, indigo is a shade of blue that *is* possible to get: poisonous monkshood *Aconitum* is one example. But turquoise, here represented as silvery blue-green to the right of blue, is not a garden colour. *Oxypetalum caeruleum* is close, but at the same time manages to appear at odds with nature.

DARKER SHADES

Inhabiting the nether end of the blue spectrum is a sombre gang. Navy-blue is a centre of lighter relief; deepest violet to its left side and petrol-blue to its right are darkly mysterious; all three are withdrawn in the extreme. Although they work with each other, these colours are difficult to pair with many others. Red and orange, lying opposite on the colour wheel, particularly defeat them.

PROPERTIES OF GREEN

❖

Green is the colour that dominates in the garden; and if flowers coloured green are rather rare (orchids are an exception), leaves abound – not only in pure green but in greens tinged silver, bronze, blue, and gold. So in the main it's foliage that we have to thank for the abundance of garden greens. Gentle and cool, green is refreshing when used alone, dramatic with red, in harmony with yellow and blue.

CONGRESS OF GREENS

Of all trees and shrubs, conifers display green in widest variety. From silver through blue-green (that approximates turquoise) to lime-green, yellow-green, and gold-green; from palest sap-green to evergreen: juniper, thuja, spruce, and cypress have them all.

PALER SHADES

The top level of green has a cool shade of turquoise-blue at far left (not a real garden colour but represented here by muscari), found in a few delphiniums and the leaves of some hostas. Olive-green in central place is a retiring hue. Lemon-green, lying to its right side, is particularly effective as a garden colour, making a good foil for blues as well as soft pastel apricot, peach, pink, and lilac.

TRUE COLOURS

Rich glossy leaf green at the heart of this square is green showing its purest form. On its cool left side, blue-green comes close to the turquoise uncommonly seen in plants. Golden green, on the warm right side of true green, will provide sunshine cheer year round in evergreens such as *Choisya ternata* 'Sundance'.

DARKER SHADES

Profound green and its close allies finish the three places in the lowest band. Sombre, matt, light-absorbing green in the centre is a colour not just of deciduous foliage but of evergreen too. Its relative dullness pleases with scarlet and orange-reds. Dark blue-green to the left is stunning in silvery mixes, while deep golden green to the right is vital enough to use alone.

PROPERTIES OF WHITE

❖

White is the colour of light, and no more visible to us in its true, pure form than is light itself. The colour that we see as white is reflected light that has other colours mixed with it in small and varying amounts. Infinite tones of white exist (white with a hint of any colour you may care to name), and the world of plants is generously blessed with them all.

Seen against other colours, white can change considerably and so different colours of leaf as well as of flower affect how we perceive white blooms. These least flamboyant inhabitants of the garden often rely on their scent to attract the creatures that pollinate them. Rose, stock, jasmine, lily, tobacco plant – the list runs on. No wonder all-white plantings are so desired.

▲ TWO-TONE FEATURE
Snowball heads of viburnum stand out brilliantly against a bank of bright new green leaves. So too do the iris (seen in the foreground at left), but they appear a warmer white, influenced by the mass of purple smoke tree leaves behind them.

◀ STARSHINE WHITE
In a boundless sea of feathery silver-blue tanacetum, white daisy flowers perch on their sinuous stalks and gleam like stars. Viciously spined aloe leaves concentrate the colour and add bold textural interest.

WHITE WITH GOLDEN GREEN

The delicate white flowers at the centre of the squares are exactly the same in each one, but each appears to be a different shade of white depending on the colour around it. Against golden green they are bright white.

WHITE WITH RICH GREEN

In the centre of glossy rich green, white seems tinged with green. Here, the colour that surrounds the white square has depth and strength, vigorous qualities that are both reflected by the white and absorbed into it.

WHITE WITH BRONZE-GREEN

Placed against bronze-green and mahogany, the white square has a much warmer feel. This effect is given by its association with red (an element of mahogany and bronze), lying on the warm side of the colour wheel.

WHITE WITH WARM GREY

A backdrop of warm grey foliage has an extraordinary, dulling effect on its centre of white flowers and makes them look beige, quite unattractive. But cool grey, in silver and silvery blues, would bring the white to life.

OPPOSITE CONTRASTS

The contrast of colour is strongest when colours that lie precisely opposite each other on the colour wheel are seen together (although when the two colours of each opposing pair are mixed together, a shade of muddy grey results).

Contrasting opposites occur between either a primary and secondary colour – which means yellow and violet, red and green, or blue and orange – or a pair of tertiary colours, in which case indigo and gold, turquoise and scarlet, or purple and chartreuse. (Page 11 explains what secondary and tertiary colours are.) In each of the pairs, the colours put against one another jump out as if they have been lit from within.

▲ QUITE CONTRARY
Orange tulips beside blue grape hyacinths make an extraordinary pairing, especially when only very little green, which would alter and diminish the effect, is visible. If a smaller quantity of one of the colours is used, the contrast is even more striking.

CONSPICUOUS ATTRACTION ▶
Against the luminous sword-like leaves of crocosmia, the brilliant red dahlia flowers seem to be on fire: the green, too, is at its most vibrant. The small amount of red to greater green gives a very lively contrast.

YELLOW & VIOLET

The same yellow is placed first with violet, which is its direct opposite on the colour wheel, and then (*far right*) with gold, a colour that is next to yellow and with which it harmonizes closely. The two yellows look completely different. Against the violet the yellow square is dazzling-bright: it leaps out to meet the eye. But against the gold it seems to withdraw and becomes much more demure.

RED & GREEN

Here is an immensely exciting pair of opposites – the heat of fiery red is set against the cool of leafy green. It seems almost impossible that this red is the same as the red that lies in the middle of harmonizing purple. On one side, the red is ablaze, but on the other seems to fade away. In the garden, the green of foliage usually offsets red, so red tends always to have even greater impact and presence.

BLUE & ORANGE

This last example of opposites made up from a primary and a secondary colour is maybe the most striking of all. The tulips and grape hyacinths opposite illustrate the garden fireworks that blue and orange provide. Seen with orange, the blue is intense and vibrant, while on the square of purple (which is blue's neighbour on the colour wheel) it looks quite dull and, indeed, arouses little interest.

HARMONY

❖

PURPLE

VIOLET

INDIGO

BLUE

TURQUOISE

GREEN

The colour wheel offers an infinite number of combinations. Those that are beautiful and at the same time very easy on the eye are the paired colours that lie close to each other. To look at the pairs, the wheel is divided into two halves. The warmer half moves clockwise from red at the apex to lime-green; the cooler half runs on from green to purple. Each pair is a harmony, yet its mood changes according to its place on the colour wheel. On the warmer half, red and scarlet, the hottest hues, make a vivid sound. Orange and gold are mellow but still sunny, yellow and lime-green a clean-cut pair. Now beginning the cooler half are green and turquoise, the latter so rare in plants that silver-grey-blue leaves take its place. Blue and indigo are the coolest hues. Violet and purple produce a feeling of composure and restraint.

PAIRS IN THE COOLER HALF

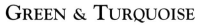

VIOLET & PURPLE

The calm reticence of violet and purple makes these for me an old-fashioned pair. Lavender and old garden roses capture their mood.

BLUE & INDIGO

These closest companions conjure a vision of deep water and intense summer skies. They are wonderful with the vitality of bright white.

GREEN & TURQUOISE

Foliage in all varieties of blue and turquoise gives a soothing view in the garden. Here, turquoise is seen as blue-green, silver-blue, or grey.

WARMER HALF

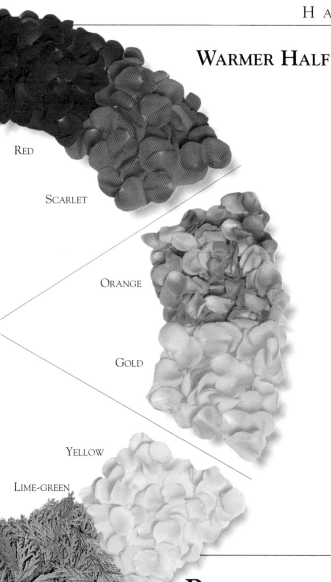

RED

SCARLET

ORANGE

GOLD

YELLOW

LIME-GREEN

ON THE SAME WAVELENGTH

You can just sense the warmth of these rich dark red tulips and orange wallflowers as you look at the picture. Their appearance in spring is so welcome! Although the colours are very brilliant, in their close harmonization they work easily with each other.

PAIRS IN THE WARMER HALF

YELLOW & LIME-GREEN

Pure and fresh, this twosome has a sharply exhilarating edge to it. An abundance of lime-green will give all the other garden colours a lift.

ORANGE & GOLD

Sweet melodies arise when orange and gold combine. They are warm and sleepy, colours of autumn that work just as well in summer heat.

RED & SCARLET

These are stunning companions, a really loud pair demanding instant attention. Not a happy mixer, red seems made for its scarlet partner.

BEAUTY IN DISCORD

❖

There are countless mixes of colour that do not rely on clear-cut contrast or harmony for their beauty. These combinations are more about juxtaposing colours in less usual – some might say, discordant – ways to produce really individual moods. A one-colour garden is not everybody's taste, but one where colours unite to bring a special atmosphere is always joyous.

If working out the mixes you like most makes you feel at sea, buy (or beg) flowers in colours you find comfortable to have around you, and make up your own combinations to see at first hand if the colours create the mood you want. The four squares at right illustrate how this is done, by bringing together unusual colours in a way I find especially beautiful and pleasing.

▲ COOL TEMPTATION
Two colours combine in this example of an offbeat pairing some gardeners might eschew, yet the mix is inspired, with pale bluish pink heads of allium that reach up toward overhanging racemes of soft yellow laburnum. Together they have irresistible appeal.

▲ SUCCESSFUL MARRIAGE
Dusty pink Achillea 'Salmon Beauty' is a gentle soul-mate for powder-blue campanulas. Softened into pastel shades of red and blue (that make a rather jumpy mix in their primary states), the colours play warm against cool in a delicately attractive way.

CHEERFUL MOOD

Red, pink, yellow, and lime-green come together in a fascinatingly warm group that raises one's spirits. Be it spring, summer, or autumn, its exotic overtones bring excitement and a sunny aspect to a border planting.

CONFIDENT MOOD

These remind me of peaches, apricots, and nectarines glowing warm and ripe from the sun. Pale pink, gold, and fresh green: the colours radiate optimism and are wonderful for high summer when roses are peaking.

PEACEFUL MOOD

Primrose-yellow, pale pink, blue, and silver are tender colours, fresh and clear. Intense blue gives a calm and peaceful feeling to the happy mix of yellow and pink, while a little silver foliage lifts it out of the ordinary.

PENSIVE MOOD

This dusky combination of dull oranges, white flecked with raspberry-pink, and metallic petrol-blue, inspires a picture of heat haze: drowsy late summer afternoons; a hammock swung from trees; a book cast lazily aside.

FORM AND TEXTURE

❖

Pure colour does not exist on its own in the garden: it is invariably influenced by other factors. Form and texture are vital links in the way we perceive colour, the mood and feel we attribute to it. Frothy white gypsophila gives a pointillist effect, a dainty haze. Massed, heavy white double peonies, stunning in their proud exquisite beauty, are a totally different matter.

Then there are leaves. Feathery and large, flat leaves; layered ones and pleated; crinkled and whorled leaves. Each has its unique form that reflects light in a different way, and even if all the leaves were one green, we would perceive as many greens as there are forms. Texture on surfaces counts too. Shiny, translucent, hairy, opaque, bloomy – all produce singular effects.

FLEETING EFFECT ▶
Spring light illuminating this acer catches the serrated edges of its leaves and, in so doing, spreads across them trails of gold. A dark green yew behind retreats into a furry pyramid, filled with shadows. Pink and lilac bluebells give an impressionistic scattering in grass below the young tree.

▼ FINE DISTINCTION
A wonderful effect is created by the same vivid fresh lime-green, here cast into two distinct forms. Frilled and finely toothed, the almost round leaves of lady's mantle have textures that work beautifully well with the feathered young fennel plumes.

◀ BRIAR PATCH

Like the finest barbed wire, bloomy silver and rust stems of ornamental blackberry Rubus cockburnianus entangle daffodils in a delicate cage. The rather eerie effect will be transformed when sprays of ferny leaves and lilac flowers emerge later on.

▼ HARD EDGE WITH SOFT

These two unrelated plants are similar in makeup, with showy bracts surrounding their flowerheads. The soft forms of pink hydrangea bracts nestling around clusters of tiny flowers look perfect with the hard, spiky, metallic-silver bracts of eryngium.

CRISP AND HAZY ▼

With its knobbed white-woolly stems and large silver-grey leaves, a grand specimen of Verbascum bombyciferum creates a robust textural partnership with the vivid crispness of variegated euonymus behind.

DISTANCE AND SCALE

❖

Colour can be used for creating effects that fool one's eye. It can be especially helpful in producing impressions of distance and scale that are at odds with reality. Cool colours and especially dark blue-greens seem further away than they are in fact. Bright warm colours are more forward so seem closer. (Pages 26 and 27 explain what the cool and warm colours are.)

To create a feeling of length in a small garden, position yellow-flowering and foliage plants at the front and have deep blue or purple flowers toward the back together with blue-green and darker green foliage. Soft and muted shades of bold tones also give an impression of distance. Their misty quality is nowhere more effective than in the creation of subtly imagined vistas.

▲ PRIMARY GAIN
Without the red poppies at its centre (try covering them with a finger), this border appears extremely deep. But reveal them and they spring toward you, carrying the surrounding view along with them, and making the border seem much less deep.

◄ DISCRETE DIFFERENCE
The brownish purple haze of smoke tree Cotinus coggygria 'Foliis Purpureis' in flower retires into the background of this informal scene, whereas the bright green of baptisia in the middle ground brings it forward, placing it close to the onlooker.

BRAIN TEASER ▶

In this picture, the plant colours invite the eye into a multi-layered effect that is both real and imagined. White and pink, seen in the mass of sedum heads with mallows and dahlias behind, put these plants to the fore. Dots of white and dusty beige draw the eye to a backdrop of interesting detail.

▼ GRAND ILLUSIONS

The separate clumps of yellow here seem to be one on top of the other, creating an impression of a rather narrow border. As background meets foreground, a strange three-dimensional image emerges, where any effect of distance has been destroyed.

SEASONAL LIGHT

❖

Each of the four seasons has its own quality of light. Transitional changes are heralded by waves of plants coming new from the earth in the endless circle of life, each set reflecting the special relationship it has with the season. The clarity of spring light is echoed in flowers of yellows, blues, and pinks. Early summer has warm, hazy morning light: it buzzes excitedly.

Midsummer revels in sun at its highest, colour at its sharp brightest. As summer progresses, a tired mood weighs down light and air: colours look jaded. Autumn hums a brief colour tune, washed with ethereal light at dawn, bathed in a honeyed evening glow. Winter, dressed now in blue crystalline light, now in grey, sparkles with spots of colour and life comes full circle.

WINTER LIGHT ▶

A pair of sombre Irish yews impress their strong outlines on the flat silver-grey light of winter, standing like stalwart bastions against the chill. Between, the pink bark of birch Betula ermanii *(whose subtlety might be lost in the profusion of summer colour) basks in the gentle wintry light.*

▼ SPRING LIGHT

The move from winter to spring is almost imperceptible: then, a sudden awareness of young green moss – illumined by clear cool shafts of light – stirs all one's senses. In the pure thin light that is spring's own gift, these tiny nodding white snowdrop heads look like glistening drops of water.

▲ SUMMER LIGHT

Alive, warm; brilliant, bright; flirtatious: all these describe qualities of midsummer light. With the sun now at its zenith, the light leaps and twirls, casting strong dark shadows as it emerges to solid blue, then sweeps across flowers in streams of gold.

◄ AUTUMN LIGHT

From the stored heat of summer, autumn releases a final joyous fling of warmth in its light. Gold, copper, rust, and burned orange form a spectrum of colour that is special to this time of year and echoed in autumn's light. Confirm the genial mood and contentment that such embered light inspires with plantings in the same hues.

DAYLIGHT TO DUSK

❖

Outside, tending to their plants, gardeners soon become familiar with the changing pattern of light through the day, and how this affects the colour of flowers and leaves. In the morning, when the sun has just risen and is at its lowest, light is apt to be cool. Then, plants have superb definition, which is why morning is such a good time to photograph the garden.

At midday, the sun has climbed to its highest point, and the light is inclined to be very flat. Because shadows are lacking, the landscape is less well defined and colours can easily appear bleached out. In the evening, the sun is again low, but the light is much warmer than in the morning. Now shadows are long, so every leaf and petal stands out in renewed sharp focus.

▲ LIGHT AT MIDDAY
With the sun high, a blaze of colour works well, because its rich palette is strong enough to compete with the flatness of reflected midday light. Muted tones, which can look lovely at morning or evening, lack interest when the light source is directly overhead.

▲ LIGHT AT DAYBREAK
The cool cutting edge of early morning light catches these grassy seed tassels excitingly; at midday they would appear dull. White plants and flowers look marvellous, clean and sharp at this time of day – worth a thought when you're creating garden schemes.

LIGHT AT EVENTIDE ▶
In the deep, warm light of evening, a multitude of greens takes on a luscious golden glow and beckoning shadows are cast over sun-warmed stones. I would like to enjoy this leafy scene every late afternoon, breathing in the mellow tranquillity it transmits.

Spring

The first bluebells are an amazing sight. Their luminous blue mirrors the colour of spring skies, spreading peace and tranquillity over grassy slopes and wooded vales through a veil of dappled sunlight and shade.

PALETTE FOR SPRING

Spring is the time of regeneration and its palette mingles the joyful colours that proclaim new life. Trees burst into a mass of translucent gold-green leaves. Grass pushes its vivid lime-green blades through the bare earth. Daffodils form drifts of limpid yellow. Blossom mixes crisp linen-whites with bright ice-pinks. Bluebells create lakes of clearest blue. And to intensify these colours, nature adds splashes of orange, scarlet, and cerise.

SPRING SKY WITH JAPANESE CHERRY BLOSSOM
Tumbling about with renewed clarity, the quality of light is at its most playful in spring as rapid changes of weather introduce, by turn, intense pale blue and scudding white to the sky. Here, a flowering cherry tree spreads a veil of snowy petals underfoot, and darting shadows illuminate both blossom and grass.

- RED *appears in the palette for spring through a wide spectrum from luminous brights to clear pastels. Blended with the other spring colours, its soft warmth anticipates summer's richness.*

- YELLOW *is jubilation in colour, breathing life into the reds, blues, whites, and greens of the season's palette. From the palest lemon to zesty vivid orange, yellow has the welcoming feel of a mood that is so well suited to this time of year.*

- BLUE, *in all its thrilling tonal variation, echoes the colours of the spring sky and of sparkling water. Set among shimmering new leaves, the calm brilliance of blue shines forth enticingly.*

- WHITE *is the colour of light and purity – symbolic meanings that make it nature's own fitting choice for the season of renewal and rebirth. Whether snowy or creamy, white adds a spark that illuminates the complete palette.*

- GREEN, *in the golden glowing form of fresh young foliage, lies at the foundation of the spring palette, a continuous backdrop that gives a soft clarity to all the other colours of this season.*

FRESH GREENS

TWO-TONE PARTNERS

EVEN THOUGH GREEN (and particularly a vivid yellowy green) is a main part of spring's palette, in cool years and climes it can make its arrival late on, as plants venture only then to put out their sparkling new leaves. Ferns, grasses, and hostas all produce prodigious quantities of lush greens. The dewy green of trees, seen at left in the graceful outlines of a Japanese maple and silver willow, is met with in many euphorbia flowers and the guelder rose. Cherish this moment, for its brief brilliance is dulled as spring wends into summer.

RELATED COLOUR SWATCH

This restful grouping mixes cooler and warmer greens in the sterile flowers and young foliage of guelder rose and hostas, and the incredible, intense golds of privet and meadowsweet leaves. Use various greens to create a relaxing focus for the eye, and a sense of tranquillity that will reassure yet stimulate, too, at the same time.

VIBURNUM OPULUS
Guelder rose.
*The mop-head
flowers of this
bushy shrub turn
almost white with age.
Red autumn leaves
add greatly to its
garden value.* ●

RESPLENDENT DISPLAY OF FOLIAGE
Around a cypress tree, fern fronds unfurl as hostas, euphorbias,
Ligularia, *and daylilies put on a leafy show. The lime-green of
shuttlecock – or ostrich – fern* Matteuccia struthiopteris *has
an exceptional vividness, paralleled by* Euphorbia seguieriana.

STARTLINGLY RENEWED APPEAL
*Grasses that can look downcast in winter wake to
lively growth. These willowy leaves of mace sedge
Carex grayi, pushing up among sweet violets, are
given an extra boost by highlights of spring sun.
Hakonechloa macra 'Aureola', also a beautiful
grass, produces fountains of striped gold-green.
Its rust-coloured flower spikes follow in autumn.*

LIGUSTRUM OVALIFOLIUM 'AUREUM'
Privet. *A dense, upright evergreen or
sometimes semi-evergreen shrub, good
as a hedging plant and for topiary.*

FILIPENDULA ULMARIA
'AUREA' Meadowsweet. *A
perennial, grown for its bright
young foliage that matures to
pale green, and with creamy
white flowers in midsummer.*

HOSTA FORTUNEI
'AUREA' Plantain lily.
*A vigorous perennial,
beloved of slugs as are
all hostas. Trumpet-
shaped purple flowers
appear in midsummer.*

OPPOSITES ATTRACT

Blue with orange; yellow with violet; red with green: it is the colours lying opposite each other in the colour wheel that produce the greatest contrasts when seen together. Such strongly vibrant colours excite and dazzle the eye, and their strength is undiminished when they're put in pairs, for opposites dovetail into natural mates. Despite the predominance of yellow in this season, many other colours are to be found – among tulips and rhododendrons in particular – that will supply a bold relief from softer spring tones.

Euphorbia characias subsp. characias Spurge. *An upright evergreen shrub with grey-green leaves that flowers from spring into early summer.*

RELATED COLOUR SWATCH

The counterpoint of primary-with-secondary colour pairs gives a thrilling perspective, a grand diversion into spring for winter-weary gardens. See how these richly red ranunculus almost leap from the page; but try hiding them with your hand and the greens seem immediately much less intense. The red would look duller, too, without the various greens on either side.

STRIKE UP THE BAND
The splayed heads of lily-flowered tulip 'Golden Duchess' form a well-considered contrast to violet-blue Muscari armeniacum. Drifts of densely massed plant colour are easily achieved with spring bulbs, but too formal a planting can look uncomfortable.

RANUNCULUS ASIATICUS Persian buttercup. *A tuberous perennial that needs shelter, with red, pink, yellow, orange, or white either single or double*
• *flowers in late spring to early summer.*

A QUIETER TUNE
Gentle contrasts can be just as effective as strong ones and make equally definite statements, but their subtlety has a more soothing effect. Here, orange Euphorbia griffithii 'Fireglow', flowering alongside a blue-purple Japanese iris in late spring, seems quite at ease. The informal mood is perfect for a wilder part of the garden.

• *BUXUS SEMPERVIRENS* Common box. *A bushy evergreen shrub or small tree reaching 5m (15ft). Its bright young growth makes a late spring treat.*

• *BUXUS SEMPERVIRENS* Common box. *Leaves of the previous years' growth have a rich green gloss on the uppersides contrasting with pale matt undersides.*

A QUIET CONTRAST

Stalwart Primula vulgaris

I FIND THE COMBINATION of yellow, the high-flying colour of spring, with purple, lilac, and bluey pink an immensely pleasing one. The contrast is not nearly so strident as when yellow is paired with violet, but the yellow inspires these shades of purple and pink and warms them with its sunny breath. Cherry blossom, hyacinths, azaleas, camellias, rhododendrons, tulips, and primroses *(see left)* all come within this colour range, and are enhanced by painterly strokes of pale and gold-green spring foliage.

RELATED COLOUR SWATCH

Spring shrubs and bulbs usually flower for rather short periods. A planting scheme that gives a succession of overlapping colours will make the most of their soft contrasts. Golden forsythia comes at the peak of the season, blooming freely on bare stems. A variegated semi-evergreen privet provides year-long colour, but shows its freshest face in late spring when new shoots appear. Purple heads of allium (an ornamental onion) and carmine-flushed tulip 'Renown' fill in the gaps.

Allium aflatunense
Ornamental onion.
A bulb flowering in late spring to early summer. The heads dry well for indoor displays.

SWEET SCENTS WITH LAVENDER
Evergreen rhododendrons have many qualities that recommend them, not least their bold foliage and fine flowers. Some gild the lily with blooms that open from distinctively coloured buds. The large primrose-yellow trusses of Exbury hybrid Rhododendron 'Crest', pictured here with an azalea, unfold from orange buds.

Ligustrum ovalifolium 'Aureum' Privet. *A semi-evergreen or evergreen shrub, needing a position in full sun for its strikingly variegated gold-and-green foliage.*

FORSYTHIA X INTERMEDIA 'SPECTABILIS'. *A deciduous shrub of spreading habit.* •

PINK PERFECTION
Single-flowered cherries are, I think, the most beautiful. It's hard to imagine any improvement on this scene of a Yoshino cherry Prunus x yedoensis *spreading a sweet-scented gauze of ice-pink blossom over naturalized narcissus 'Fortune'.*

• TULIPA 'RENOWN'
Single late. *A reliable late spring or very early summer bulb, supplying in each flower a muted contrast of carmine-red and creamy yellow.*

ESSENTIAL SPRING

GOLD, YELLOW, CREAM, AND WHITE: in all their aspects of harmony, clarity, and purity, these are the colours that signal the arrival of spring. Their shining brightness spreads through the land in blossom and bloom, while trees break into tender new foliage that is lime sharp in its intensity. Clearest blue skies, lightly broken by hurrying clouds, smile on this conspiracy of colour, giving the yellows and whites even more luminous power and brilliance.

POLYGONATUM COMMUTATUM
Great Solomon's seal. *A leafy perennial bearing demure, bell-shaped white flowers in small clusters during late spring.*

TULIPA 'OSTARA'
Double late. *A peony-flowered bulb blooming in late spring.*

TULIPA 'GOLDEN APELDOORN'
Darwin hybrid. *A bulb with large single flowers from mid- to late spring.*

RELATED COLOUR SWATCH

High spring sunshine bursts forth in this group that combines the rich translucent yellow tones of single 'Golden Apeldoorn' and double 'Ostara' tulips with Great Solomon's seal and the clear pale green young leaves of *Euphorbia polychroma*. Broom adds its joyful golden spires and breathes a honeyed scent besides.

CYTISUS x PRAECOX 'ALLGOLD' Common broom. *A deciduous shrub with palest green leaves and masses of golden pea-like flowers in late spring.* •⎯

• EUPHORBIA POLYCHROMA Spurge. *A bushy perennial with fresh yellow-green foliage. Loose heads of yellow flowers appear over a long period during the spring months.*

FLOWERY DRIFTS AMONG GRASS
Gold and white narcissus 'Fortune' and 'Kilworth' nod before a fountain of brilliant yellow Forsythia x intermedia; *for a softer effect, try* F. suspensa. *These narcissus naturalize well in grass, which is best left unmown until their foliage has died down.*

A PLANT FOR MOIST PLACES
Skunk cabbage – Lysichiton camtschatcensis – seems a sad name for this beautiful perennial that likes to grow beside, or even with its feet in, water. Its large spathes of cream-flushed-yellow emerge in spring before the rich green leaves unfold.

◄ SPREADING GROUND COVER
Fragile-looking windflower Anemone blanda *is at its most lovely in the white form nestling here before a low-growing narcissus, 'Jack Snipe'. Plant anemones in a spot where they can run wild: once established they soon become invasive.*

ZESTY WELCOME ►
The stronger colour tones of spring are one of its exhilarating surprises. In this classic combination of azure, emerald, gold, and deep orange, light appears to dance over the landscape, imparting a vibrancy to narcissus 'Ambergate' that is so very much a mark of early spring.

ESSENCE OF THE SEASON ▲
Demure, delicate, and refreshing, this grouping conveys a mood of pure spring, with variegated evergreen Euonymus fortunei *'Emerald and Gold' backing the silver-veined leaf rosettes and serenely reflexed flower petals of* Erythronium *'White Beauty'.*

IN A LEAFY WOODED GLEN ▲
Yellow azalea Rhododendron luteum *shines out wondrously among the lime-green foliage of trees dappled with the tenuous rays of early sunshine. Its flowers, resembling those of a large honeysuckle, infuse the air with nutmeg and clove scents.*

SUBTLE WARMTH

HELLEBORUS WITH NARCISSUS

ONE OF MY favourite groupings is a range taken from the warm side of the colour wheel. Yet even more than the colours themselves, the yellows and oranges, reds and purples, it's the subtle variations on them – encompassing peaches and cream, apricot with ice-pink, plum set against gold – that are such a delight. These produce extraordinary effects that are a little bit unusual but still easy on the eye: the spotted deep pink Lenten roses and daffodils *(left)* make a wonderful marriage. Whatever the weather, these colour schemes spread a warm and joyous prospect.

RELATED COLOUR SWATCH

This marvellously mellow suite is made from five late spring bulbs and shrubs. The spires of fritillary have a deep red translucent quality to their chocolate-brown coloration, which is nearly matched in the bicoloured broom, and faintly echoed by the pink margins of the azalea petals. Frilled and fringed salmon parrot tulips bring their bright colourful edge to the scheme, while the aptly named *Spiraea japonica* 'Goldflame' binds it together with tender foliage in orange-reds and gold.

FRITILLARIA PERSICA 'ADIYAMAN' Fritillary. *A bulb flowering through the season. The stems are clothed with narrow grey-green leaves.*

SPLASHED WITH SUN
Royal fern Osmunda regalis, which can reach a stately height of 2m (6ft), unfurls its great fronds in a brilliant swath of late spring sunshine. Behind, the coral trumpets of Rhododendron 'May Day' spread a warm glow against their dark green leaves.

MELODIOUS TONES
Growing in their preferred moist spot, a group of perennial candelabra primulas exhibits a broad variety of colours in this range. From yellows to golds through burnt orange to mauves and faded pinks: it's a lovely sunny-looking, uplifting mix, and the primulas' own rosetted pale green leaves serve to highlight and set off the other colours.

RHODODENDRON 'CECILE' Knap Hill azalea. A small deciduous shrub. The large trumpet-shaped flowers are borne in late spring.

TULIPA 'SALMON PARROT' Parrot group. A bulb that produces its typical frilly petalled flowers in late spring.

SPIRAEA JAPONICA 'GOLDFLAME'. An upright deciduous shrub with orange-red young leaves becoming bright yellow then green.

CYTISUS SCOPARIUS 'PALETTE' Broom. A deciduous shrub bearing pea-like flowers along leafy arching branches during late spring.

COOL COMPANIONS

SHADES OF COLOUR in cooler tones seem to be especially suited to this time of year. In this fresh, reserved combination of pale blue-pink and lilac, powder pink, mauve, white, silver, and cream, each colour adds its own clear voice to produce an appropriate mood of serenity in the garden – a period of composure before rising temperatures stimulate more vibrant colours. Promote this feel of calm continuity with plants that step easily from spring to summer. In this range, there are many lilacs, and azaleas too, that straddle the seasons.

RELATED COLOUR SWATCH

A perfection of pinks in this collection of shrubs and perennial snakeweed (or bistort) inspires a cheerfully relaxed mood and would make a splendid planting to cover both the end of spring and the start of summer. Weigelas often add to their bounty – and value in the garden – by producing another show later in summer.

SOFT HUES WITH STRONG ACCENTS
The neat daisy heads of Bellis perennis *'Pomponette' have an attractive woolly-ball texture that enhances their shades of soft pink and white. With them, the blue-green leaves and fringed magenta flowers of a late-flowering tulip form an easy rapport.*

WEIGELA FLORIDA. A strong-growing deciduous shrub. To maintain vigour, cut back after flowering.

POLYGONUM
BISTORTA
'SUPERBUM'
Snakeweed,
bistort. *A
perennial that
can become
invasive.*

LIGHT-HEARTED PARTNERS
*For the smaller garden, I greatly favour
azaleas in understated pastels over those
in bold strong tones that can overwhelm.
Here, Rhododendron 'Sir Edmund' is
paired with R. 'Lavender Girl' in an
ensemble of delicately retiring beauty.*

SYRINGA 'ESTHER
STALEY' Lilac. *A
deciduous shrub. Red
buds open to scented
flowers from mid-
spring to early
summer.*

RHODODENDRON
'PURPLE TRIUMPH'
Vuyk hybrid azalea.
*An evergreen shrub
needing shelter from
cold winds and some
shade. Profuse, large
single flowers appear
during late spring.*

WHITE WITH RED

COMPANION PLANTING

WHEN RED – the most dazzling of all the colours – is viewed against white, it takes on an almost cool light: it's as if some of the heat has been drawn out of it. And white seems to become even more pure and clean in the presence of red, as the strong primary intensifies its clarity. In the garden other colours, particularly of foliage and ground and sky, divert such simple relationships. Even so the principles apply: the ox-eye daisies (*left*) look so much brighter for the lone red campion stalk – a natural association of plants in a wild part of the garden.

RELATED COLOUR SWATCH

Nestled in between flowering stems of vanilla-scented Mexican orange blossom and dainty spiraea, deep red dark-spotted blooms of rhododendron 'Wilgen's Ruby' withdraw into a rose-pink glow that throws luminous highlights over the creamy whites and greens. In this partnership of bold contrasts, each one of the colours lends its most positive aspects to enhance the others.

BRILLIANT WHITE LIGHT
Against the rich red trusses of Rhododendron *'Elizabeth' and its abundant glossy sea-green foliage,* R. *'Beauty of Littleworth' blooms white tinged cool blue. These evergreen hybrids are best planted in the dappled shade of trees, but not underneath them.*

CHOISYA TERNATA
Mexican orange blossom. *An evergreen shrub that flowers in late spring, often repeating in mild autumn weather.*

Summer snowflake Leucojum aestivum *– oddly named, for it's a spring-flowering bulb – provides a dazzling foreground to overhanging branches of* Camellia japonica *'Julia Drayton', heavy with large crimson flowers that vary from rose-form to formal double. Both plants will grow happily and thrive in acid soil, given a lightly shaded position.*

RHODODENDRON 'WILGEN'S RUBY'. *A mid- to late spring-flowering evergreen shrub.*

SPIRAEA 'ARGUTA' Bridal wreath, Foam of May. *A dense deciduous shrub wreathed in clusters of tiny white flowers in late spring.*

◄ DELICATE ALLIANCE
Flowering in mid-spring, a willow-leaved
Magnolia salicifolia *casts veils of starry*
white across a misty wooded background.
Its fragility is further emphasized by the
almost tropical warmth and richness of
the deep crimson rhododendron blooms.

GENTLE PROVOCATION ►
White with orange-red makes for a softer
effect – one that's still exciting but a little
less intense. These tufted great umbrellas
of crown imperial Fritillaria imperialis
look really magnificent beside Narcissus
'Merlin', whose slightly ruffled central
cups echo the colour of the fritillary bells.

▼ CHANGE OF PACE
Narcissus provide many opportunities for
variations on the theme. 'Sempre Avanti'
brings dots of buff-apricot to this planting
that blur the margin of contrast between
the cardinal-red of Tulipa *'Ile de France'*
and the vivid greens of leaves and grass.

Summer

In lovely, varied textures and colours that are both vivid, soft, and subtle, a meadow planting sings out the glory of the season. At no other time of year is the gardener presented with such a rich choice of bounteous gifts.

PALETTE FOR SUMMER

Summer releases the energy of plants in a
rush of colour, and gardeners are spoiled
for choice. Glorious combinations clamour
against lush verdant greens. Contrasts and
harmonies sing with myriad voices: demurely
in white, cream, lilac, and ice-pink; warmly
in the sunniest of yellows, oranges, and golds;
powerfully in vibrant scarlet and vermilion.
And as the season wears on, the song changes
to brooding tones of indigo and wine-red.

EARLY PROMISE FOR A FEAST OF COLOUR
*Pale summer morning light tracks down the misty pinks of lilac
and ornamental onion heads, leaving blue columbine in partial
shade. A softly harmonizing mix emerges among the rich greens
of herbaceous foliage, punctuated by darker spires of Irish yew.*

● BLUES *in summer's palette lean often toward the red end of the spectrum. This leaning makes them blend especially well with the pinks and paler purples that dominate the early part of the season.*

● YELLOW *has a depth to its rich colour tone that reflects the increasing warmth of the sun. All through the season, it's in harmony with orange and golden greens and forms exciting contrasts when used with violet and bluish pinks.*

● ORANGE *is at its freshest and most lively in summer, lying sociably between red and yellow. Used with this pair, the effect is warm and friendly. In small amounts with pastel lilac, pale pink, and lime-green, its jewel-like quality shines through.*

● PINKS *appear in varying forms. Early peony pastels, gathering momentum in the lurid tones of high summer phlox, fade in the glow of first chrysanthemums. All blend happily together with the palette's other colours.*

● REDS *speak with a strong, deep velvety voice during the summer months. Luminous and startling against foliage greens, reds are dulled and forfeit their vitality in blue and violet partnerships.*

HARMONY OF RICH PINKS

GENTEEL *DIANTHUS BARBATUS*

W ITH SUMMER COME a host of flowers in shades set between red and purple on the colour wheel. Pinks in particular go on display, and their major role in the garden lasts all season. It's easy to plan a scheme that encompasses these related colours, from true primary red spreading out through fuchsia-pink to cherry-red, cool ice-pink, lilac, and mauve: sweet William (*left*) contrives such a grouping on its own. There is a safety in harmony that inspires confidence and you can be sure that the mood of such a planting will always be beautiful to behold in a gently undemanding way.

RELATED COLOUR SWATCH

A swath of bright rich pinks will shimmer in the sun of summer. All these pinks are composed of red with the addition of either blue, black, or white. Textures play a strong part and enhance the interest in single-colour plantings. The wavy velvet ruffles of *Celosia* are echoed here in both the stripy pale pink mallow petals and the layered pompons of globe amaranth.

GOMPHRENA GLOBOSA Globe amaranth. *A bushy annual with pink, purple, orange, yellow, or white flowers from mid-to late summer.*

COMPLEMENTARY FORMS
The blue-pinks and pale mauves of daisy-like cineraria flowers harmonize well with the dark leaves of hazel Corylus maxima 'Purpurea' in both texture and tone. Boldly outlined but subtly patterned and with a rich depth of colour, the foliage is a lovely complement to the delicate forms and soft hues of the flowers.

FLEETING APPEAL
Biennial foxglove Digitalis purpurea *has tall and undulating spikes of bell-shaped flowers in various pinks as well as white, all with dark-spotted throats. Cut off the stems after the short flowering period in early summer and you will be rewarded with a second showing of smaller spikes.*

CELOSIA ARGENTEA VAR. CRISTATA *Cockscomb. An upright perennial grown as an annual, flowering in late summer. It includes many dwarf cultivars.* •

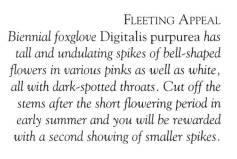

• LAVATERA TRIMESTRIS 'SILVER CUP' *Mallow. An erect, branching annual that flowers successively through summer into autumn.*

MASSED PLANTING ▶
Valerian Centranthus ruber *will grow with disarming ease in the most curious spots: the apparently inhospitable cracks between paving slabs, or in stone walls, are ideal domains. Here, an abundance of its pink and brick-red flowers creates a satisfyingly integrated depth of colour.*

◀ TWO IN ONE
Primula vialii *produces its own colour harmony in rich scarlet buds atop a ruff of mauve open flowers. Grown close to water – it likes a moist soil – the conical vivid spikes look wondrous, poised above clumps of their upright pale green leaves.*

▼ ENERGETIC PARTNERSHIP
The intense vermilion of campion Silene coeli-rosa *'Fire King' sits in bold accord with purple-flowering* Verbena venosa. *Peeking up through the tangle, rain daisy* Dimorphotheca pluvialis *highlights the strong colours with tiny specks of white.*

◀ AGREEABLE CHOICE

Slender spires of densely clustered lupin flowers have immediate textural as well as colourful impact. Resplendent in an array of tones that runs from yellow to orange through red and pink to lilac and blue, bicoloured Russell hybrids are sure to find a place in harmonizing schemes.

▼ PICTURE OF HARMONY

Shades of pink that contain overtones of blue combine particularly well with lilac hues. The delicate coloration of Echium vulgare is here reflected in the clear blue rose-pink Cosmos bipinnatus, accented by yellow centres. Rosettes of frilled and wavy-edged clarkia flowers and fine-cut frothy cosmos foliage set off the picture.

▲ EXTENDED BOUNDARIES
The magnificent white-striped blooms of
Rosa mundi *(Rosa gallica 'Versicolor')*
are muddled only in high summer among
Rosa *'Mrs Anthony Waterer', flowering*
through the season. Their vivid crimson,
combined with mauve catmint Nepeta x
faassenii, *stretches harmony to the limit.*

◀ TRANQUIL VALE
A well-contrived but still informal study
in related colours. Clustered, dusty pink
Phuopsis stylosa *heads that lean faintly*
toward blue enliven the quieter voices of
lavender-hued catmint Nepeta 'Six Hills
Giant', pinkish purple ornamental onion
Allium christophii, *and dark maroon-*
red sweet William Dianthus barbatus.

COTTAGE CACOPHONY

INFORMAL AND INTIMATE, the cottage garden – once a utilitarian
planting of vegetables, herbs, and fruits – evolved over centuries
into an exuberant, haphazard mix of edible and decorative plants.
Now, to recreate the impression of cozy ease, we tend to plan our
cottage gardens, combining old-fashioned favourites in colourful
variety with a liberal sprinkling of herbs, but often excluding the
fruits and vegetables. Unsophisticated
plants will furnish the
right feeling of calm
disorder, set in close
groups so as to look
casually self-seeded.

ALCHEMILLA MOLLIS
Lady's mantle. *A perennial
that flowers in midsummer.
Pesticide-free baby leaves
are good in salads.*

*CARTHAMUS
TINCTORIUS*
Safflower. *A prickly
leaved annual. Oil
from its seeds is rich in
essential fatty acids.*

MONARDA DIDYMA 'BLUE
STOCKING' Bergamot. *A
summer perennial
whose flowers
and leaves are
both fragrant.*

RELATED COLOUR SWATCH

This medley of golden orange with pinks and yellows conveys a distinctly cottage-garden mood. Bergamot, safflower, lady's mantle, statice, larkspur: their names ring sweet with herbal references, and the profusion of soft colour shades and textural variation provides two ingredients that are an essential part of the look.

CONSOLIDA AMBIGUA 'ROSAMUND' Larkspur. A tall annual with many other cultivars in shades of blue or white as well as pink.

LIMONIUM SINUATUM 'GOLDCREST' Statice. Perennial grown as an annual. Late summer flowers, also in white, blue, pink, and purple, are excellent dried.

REASON TO BE CHEERFUL
Lacking the strident contrast of violets and blues, this jovial mix of white ox-eye daisies and spires of purple salvia, planted amid brilliant orange alstroemeria Ligtu Hybrids and yellow evening primrose, has a calm optimism to brighten the dullest of days.

QUIET COMPOSITION
Subdued tones evoke the tranquil spirit of a cottage garden and blend with the pink-washed shutters of this charming clapboard home. Cool purple catmint Nepeta x faassenii and sprawling mignonette Reseda lutea climb up by Rosa 'Little White Pet', while mallow Lavatera olbia 'Rosea' taps at the windowpane.

◀ EVER-CHANGING VARIETY
*At the base of a dry-stone wall, a tumble
of self-seeded plants (including valerian,
verbascum, and daisy) produces just the
haphazard mix that every cottage garden
needs: it's a wonderful combination that
has great charm. Every year, it will look
a bit different, and bring a fresh surprise.*

▼ A LAVISH SPREAD
*Much of a cottage garden's character lies
in an abundance of colours and textures.
Here, red and coral poppies have woven
themselves in among violet campanulas,
creamy yellow* Sisyrinchium striatum,
and Chrysanthemum frutescens *'Pink
Australian', a newish sort of marguerite
but with an appealing old-fashioned feel.*

▲ CONTROLLED CONFUSION
Less informal, in a refined colour palette of peach, orange, and white, this flowery spread still conjures the mood. Roses are an important feature, grown as shrubs or over walls or arches, or climbing through tree branches. Surrounding shorter-lived daylilies, the double blooms of 'Elizabeth Harkness' will scent the air for months.

RANDOM PLANTING ▶
The single or double cups of annual field poppy Papaver rhoeas Shirley Series *are in shades from white to ice-pink to coral and bright red. Give this delicate beauty freedom to self-seed where it likes: here, scattered through* Gladiolus communis *subsp.* byzantinus *and purple vetch.*

EVENING GLOW

W HEN THE AFTERNOON draws to an end, and the sun dips low in the sky, colours take on and reflect a new light. Velvety reds and their closest relatives begin to glow with a luminous inner warmth. Valuing this daily gift, I like to grow flowering plants near and around an outdoor sitting and eating place (where it is good to go to relax after hours of work), in an uplifting and revitalizing mix of crimson, scarlet, coral, and vivacious reds. For hard-paved areas, this colour range includes many annuals that will thrive in containers, which can be moved about to create eye-catching effects.

MONARDA DIDYMA 'CAMBRIDGE SCARLET' Bergamot. A clump-forming perennial with deeply veined, aromatic leaves. The rich red flowers appear from mid- to late summer.

RELATED COLOUR SWATCH

This mix of perennial bergamot with two selections of bush rose and annual antirrhinum produces a glowing quartet of dusky companions in myriad reds. Carefully chosen roses give stupendous colour for a long period, although some make untidy shrubs. Introducing other plants for textural and complementary colour interest besides will ensure a scheme that delights for months.

FLUSHED WITH WARMTH
Rose 'Living Fire' is so aptly named: in the lengthening shadows the flowers appear to burn against its gleaming dark foliage. It is most effective set toward the front of a bed and behind a mound of blue-purple, such as this planting of lavender, 'Grappenhall'.

PLAY OF LIGHT AND SHADOW
The salmon- and red-pink blooms of climbing rose 'Aloha' furnish a custom-mix of colour in low as well as brighter light. Sweet alyssum Lobularia maritima – spreading white below – echoes their delicious fragrance, and flowers all summer long.

ANTIRRHINUM MAJUS PRINCESS SERIES
Snapdragon. A perennial, grown as an annual, with bicoloured flowers from early summer until autumn.

ROSA 'NATIONAL TRUST'
Hybrid tea. A bush rose producing masses of lightly scented double flowers from summer to autumn.

ROSA 'NORWICH CASTLE'
Floribunda. A free-flowering bush rose that fades from deep coppery orange to apricot.

◄ AT THE CLOSE OF DAY
Pushing upright from a sea of cut-leaved foliage, the brilliant gaudy scarlet blooms of Papaver orientalis 'Allegro Viva' are caught, gleaming, in late afternoon sun. Lobelia cardinalis would make a show of equal fire and throws splendid sword-shaped purple leaves into the bargain.

RADIANT WARMTH ►
There is no missing the penetrating pink of phlox 'Sir John Salmon' and its near-fluorescent quality as dazzling sunbeams flood over. Verbascum rises against giant thistles behind the phlox, while evergreen Jerusalem sage shines in mounds before.

▲ GENTLE PURPLE BATHED WITH LIGHT
The blazing red heads of Lychnis chalcedonica are satisfyingly juxtaposed with slender stems of purple sage Salvia x sylvestris, which might otherwise appear a rather sombre colour. Deep red rose 'The Herbalist' would also suit the mood of quiet restraint.

▲ GLOWING HUES JOSTLE FOR ATTENTION
This border sings out cheerily against the shadows of smoke tree Cotinus coggygria 'Foliis Purpureis': the lack of light presents no obstacle. Tobacco plant, verbena, antirrhinum, penstemon, dahlia, and amaranth vie with each other to dominate the scene.

TRANQUIL VISTAS

ALLIUM, AQUILEGIA, NEPETA

SOFT COLOUR TONES and delicacy of texture in flowers and foliage is a most helpful combination when creating a scheme that takes in any kind of view. It may be a path, a vista through to fields or the sea, across a valley, or just to a wild planting: the idea is to get from your view that lazy feeling that spells somnolent late afternoons at the peak of summer. At left, feathery spheres of ornamental onion lift up their heads among nodding columbines, fade into a filigree of airy catmint spires, and draw the eye back to settle on hedging of darkest green. All come together in a three-layered harmony of dreamy restfulness.

RELATED COLOUR SWATCH

Branching spires and plumes in gentle shades suggest, by their natural forms, a mood of languorous content. Here, milkweed, love-in-a-mist with its delicately cut foliage, loose flowerheads of aromatic dill, floribunda rose 'Ainsley Dickson', and delphinium 'Loch Leven' conjure the atmosphere in mellow golds, misty pinks, smoke-blues, veiled creams, and muted foliage greens.

ASCLEPIAS INCARNATA
Milkweed. *A hardy tuberous perennial. The stems exude a milky sap, giving rise to the common name.*

NIGELLA DAMASCENA
'MISS JEKYLL' Love-in-a-mist. *A summer annual that grows fast. Decorative seed pods follow the flowers.*

INVITATION TO A PEACEFUL PLACE
Grazing a stone-flagged path, this deep border fades away in a pink tamarisk mist to distant hedges and trees. Smoke tree, tall thistles, and rose 'The Fairy' join with Jerusalem sage Phlomis fruticosa, artemisia, and phlox to bring about the desired effect.

HILLS AND VALLEYS

Deep sultry colours leading to paler ones present a layered view through to fields. For such a scheme of roses, select shrubby varieties that will grow to the right height – with some forming small mounds and others to rise taller at the sides, an impression of cleft hills is given at once. Planted between the roses, low artemisias and lavenders obscure their stems and fill the air with the drowsy hum of bees.

DELPHINIUM 'LOCH LEVEN'. *A perennial with generously endowed flower spikes to 1m (3ft) tall.*

ANETHUM GRAVEOLENS Dill. *An annual herb that has edible flowers, leaves, and seeds.* ●

ROSA 'AINSLEY DICKSON' Floribunda. *A vigorous summer to autumn selection.* ●

▲ HOSPITABLE HAVEN
*Carefully organized disarray invests this
sunny garden room with a feeling of filmy
space; and the aromatic foliage spreading
beneath slender rocket and columbine in
pink and purple is a joy to walk through.
Violet iris and bold* Euphorbia characias
draw the eye subtly toward a dark hedge.

GENTLE SASHAY ▶
*Resembling clusters of fruit-drops in dusty
hues, plumed lupin spikes emerge from a
tangle of foliage and rough grass to sway
elegantly into the distance. These Russell
strain are a popular hybrid that produces
its best colours on light, not too rich soil.*

◀ SEASCAPE WITH PLANTS
*Pelargoniums of all sorts; long-flowering
blue marguerite* Felicia amelloides; *and
graceful Madonna lilies with poppies and
gazanias beckon the eye down steps to the
seashore: a pointillist planting of annuals
in an idyllic setting of unrivalled allure.*

BLUE SUMMER MAGIC

PENETRATING BLUE POPPY

I THINK THAT BLUE is the most special colour in the garden. There are not many flowers with good blue colouring (which perhaps explains their favoured place), although there are very many often described as blue that are in fact purple- or lavender-blue: shown left, *Meconopsis betonicifolia* is a true blue of outstanding quality. Coming from the cool side of the colour wheel and traditionally associated with spiritual things, blue conjures a mood of innermost peace. It's a delight with pink, cream, lemon-yellow, and silver, but dull and flat in red and purple partnerships.

RELATED COLOUR SWATCH

This quartet of plants has an inspired touch and is no less magical for its lack of a true blue. At far right, sea holly *Eryngium alpinum* has metallic silver-blue bracts reflected in the white eyes of delphinium 'Blue Nile'. Between and to the left, agapanthus and cornflowers (caught in shafts of light) add shades of mauver blue.

CENTAUREA CYANUS
Cornflower. *A branching, fast-growing annual with flowers in reds, pinks, purples, and white as well as blue through summer and into early autumn.*

MAGNIFICENT MASS PLANTING
Grown in neutral and alkaline soils, the flattened open heads of lacecap Hydrangea macrophylla 'Blue Wave' will bloom lilac or pink. Only acid soil encourages such an incredible exhibition of pure blue, which will last for a long period from midsummer.

STATELY REGALIA ON DISPLAY
Delphiniums reign supreme in all their rich variety of blue. Lit from behind, delphinium 'Fenella' has a superb depth of colour, overwashed with purple and intensified by each flower's central black boss.

DELPHINIUM ELATUM 'BLUE NILE'. A perennial that bears its semi-double flowers on spikes to 69cm (27in) tall.

AGAPANTHUS CAMPANULATUS. A clump-forming perennial producing strong erect stems of profuse rounded flower clusters.

ERYNGIUM ALPINUM Sea holly. A perennial with deeply toothed foliage and, in summer, conical flowers surrounded by dramatic feathered silver-blue bracts.

◀ PEACE OFFERING

A gift of nature: in cracks in stone steps, china-blue speedwell Veronica prostrata *and pale lavender bellflower* Campanula garganica *have seeded themselves into a colourscape of rare magic. Lady's mantle* Alchemilla mollis, *in frothy lime-green, enlivens the otherwise very cool effect.*

BRIGHTER VISION ▶

The luxuriant cream-striped leaves of Iris laevigata *'Variegata' make a background for its flowers that throws into relief their beautiful soft lilac-blue, showing them off to perfection. This beardless Japanese iris will often flower again in early autumn.*

▲ BOON COMPANIONS

Apricot-pink rose 'Paul Shirville' casts its sensuous soft warmth over the cool blue of love-in-a-mist Nigella damascena. *Sweet scented daylily* Hemerocallis *'Prairie Sunset', with* Consolida ambigua *'Blue Spire', could make just such convivial partners.*

▲ GRAPHIC GROUP

Sculpted out of steely blue, sea holly Eryngium x oliverianum *is a striking sight in late summer with its egg-shaped flowerheads and delicately spiked silver bracts. Its deep-cut leaves and those of variegated New Zealand flax emphasize the dramatic effect.*

MUTED HUES

WHEN SUMMER BESTOWS the pleasure of its balmiest days, the fresh and hazy early morning air seems to shimmer with a watchful charge. It's a time of great beauty, when even bold colours look muted. The mood is one of expectation and drowsy optimism. I like to recreate this feeling, so that it need not rely on either weather or time of day, by using a misty palette restricted to pinks, lilacs, mauves, purples, and silvery greys. Delicate plant textures complement the subtle colour range and help to support the illusion.

PHLOX PANICULATA 'SKYLIGHT'. An upright perennial flowering in late summer. It is best grown in a rich, moist but well-drained soil.

RELATED COLOUR SWATCH

This group will send a cool, refreshing breeze wafting over the most sultry landscape. Layers of frilled petals and feathery spires are the perfect textural adjunct to the understated lavenders, deep mauves, warm pinks, and silver-green seen in phlox, *Lavandula angustifolia* 'Hidcote', *Dianthus* 'Doris', and evergreen santolina.

SALUTATION TO THE DAY
Placed against heads of purple coneflower Echinacea purpurea *'Robert Bloom',* Perovskia atriplicifolia *sends its sage-scented silvery foliage and blue-grey flower spires curling toward the sky like ribbons of smoky mist at dawn. Sub-shrub* P. atriplicifolia *will bloom to mid-autumn, outlasting the summer coneflowers.*

MODESTLY SUPPORTING STRUCTURES
A planting of mauve Geranium 'Johnson's Blue' lies agreeably quiescent behind close-knit clumps of pink Dianthus 'Little Jock' with their dainty, spice-perfumed flowers. Spiky silver-green dianthus leaves and the hard grey stone of the path anchor both plants in their stronger textures.

LAVANDULA ANGUSTIFOLIA
'HIDCOTE' Lavender. *An evergreen shrub that forms a dense mound and is covered with flowers from mid- to late summer.*

DIANTHUS 'DORIS'
Modern pink. *A compact perennial. The abundant flowers are deeply scented and excellent for cutting.*

SANTOLINA CHAMAECYPARISSUS
Cotton lavender. *An evergreen shrub with bright yellow, button-like flowerheads in mid- and late summer, and aromatic foliage.*

◄ A FANCIFUL VISION
Elemental colours mix in a hushed reverie of rose quartz meadowsweet Filipendula rubra, *steely blue bellflower* Campanula lactiflora, *and the large bronze leaves of plantain* Plantago major *'Rubrifolia'.*

GOSSAMER LIGHT ►
An ornamental onion bears its violet-grey pompons aloft through a mist of artichoke Cynara scolymus. *Edging to meet them, the fluffy floss-pink spikes of steeplebush* Spiraea tomentosa *will keep their dried brown flowers right until winter sets in.*

▼ CURIOUS COMPANIONS
In an unexpected yet comfortable alliance of forms, elegant fluted mallow Lavatera trimestris *'Pink Beauty' grows beside the elongated flowerheads and greenish white bracts of sea holly* Eryngium giganteum.

SERENE IN WHITE

WHITE IS THE COLOUR of true light, and has always been regarded as the symbol of purity and innocence. It is also refined and elegant. No wonder that we should choose to plant entire gardens with all-white flowers. Against the glorious diversity of foliage greens, white stands out distinctively. On hot summer days, white flowers chasten the sun's glare with their cool freshness; in shade, they speak with inspiring eloquence. Even a small part of a garden planted in white will lend its composed beauty to the whole. As an added pleasure, there are many white flowers that count sweet perfume among their other charms.

MYRTUS LUMA Myrtle. An evergreen shrub that is in flower from mid- to late summer.

RELATED COLOUR SWATCH

White flowers look particularly good among differing greens. Dark green makes them look spotlessly white, while gold foliage gives them a touch of warmth. Use a mix of texture, associating dots of tiny flowers with larger-petalled ones, spheres with spires. Here *Myrtus luma*, an aromatic myrtle, is placed alongside mallow, with *Ammi visnaga* and an intensely scented phlox.

SHORT BUT SWEET
Philadelphus 'Belle Etoile', sadly beloved of aphids, more than makes up for this shortcoming with a profusion of most fragrant flowers opening among still-fresh young foliage in early summer. A curtain of gold- and blue-greens behind intensifies its beauty.

BASKING IN REFLECTED GLORY
Love-in-a-mist Nigella damascena *'Persian Jewels'* blooms blue or pink, besides the dazzling white that is here so effectively paired with silver artemisia. Sweet rocket Hesperis matronalis *and* Geranium clarkei *'Kasmir White' would also sit well in a planting of this planned cottagey type.*

LAVATERA TRIMESTRIS
'MONT BLANC'
Mallow. *A branching annual with abundant flowers from summer to early autumn.*

AMMI VISNAGA. *A self-seeding annual, related to Anthriscus. Flowers are borne in mid- to late summer among feathery aromatic foliage.*

PHLOX PANICULATA
'FUJIYAMA'. *An herbaceous perennial, also listed as 'Mount Fuji', with flowers in late summer.*

IMMACULATE WHITE ▶

Rosa *'Wedding Day'*, *nearly clouding an iron cupola, furnishes a bountiful display in early summer with* Lychnis coronaria *'Alba', tradescantias, and cistus. Stately delphiniums, just visible, appear behind.*

◀ FLOWERY TRELLIS

In stalky fountains, Crambe cordifolia *(a delicate garden sea kale) bursts above a mound of hostas and its own leaves. It makes a gracious partner for white roses: the bourbon 'Boule de Neige' and rugosa 'Schneezwerg' are two of my favourites.*

▼ COOL COMPOSURE

A contained planting of Osteospermum *'Whirligig', golden-leaved* Helichrysum petiolare, *and* Lilium longiflorum *with* Nicotiana alata *'Lime Green'. Tendrils of everlasting pea wave airily over them.*

VIVACIOUS YELLOWS

CLEAR AND FRESH, yellow spells out a stirring affirmation of life's excitement whenever it appears. At this time of year we see yellow and its close companions gold, pale orange, and lime-green playing a vivacious, even audacious part, reflecting the sun's brilliance on bright days, triumphing gloriously over dull ones. Place yellow flowers and golden foliage together for a dual feel-good effect that is sure to lift the weariest of spirits.

LIGUSTRUM OVALIFOLIUM 'AUREUM' Variegated privet. A semi-evergreen shrub that needs a site in full sun to keep its variegation.

RELATED COLOUR SWATCH

This joyful association in gold and yellow is just right for a sunny position. Many yellow plants have an easy simplicity that cheers without inviting restless frenzy. Here, variegated privet foliage merges into floribunda roses, set between rich golden aromatic yarrow heads and soft-plumed thistles with loosestrife spires beside.

GILT-EDGED SPLENDOUR
Towering stems of mullein Verbascum bombyciferum *grow up rapidly from their rosetted silver-grey evergreen leaves, and look particularly spectacular against an emerald green hedge. Daylily* Hemerocallis *'Golden Orchid' in front adds a mellow warmth.*

ISLAND IN A SEA OF GOLD
In a feathery bank, white Crambe cordifolia *and silver artichoke foliage rise tall behind a golden lemon sea of yarrow* Achillea 'Coronation Gold' *and whorled Jerusalem sage* Phlomis fruticosa.

ROSA 'HARVEST FAYRE'
Floribunda. *A shrub rose flowering from midsummer until late autumn.* ●

CENTAUREA MACROCEPHALA
Knapweed. *A clump-forming perennial.* ●

ACHILLEA FILIPENDULINA 'GOLD PLATE' Yarrow. *A tall perennial growing to* ● *1.2m (4ft) or more.*

LYSIMACHIA VULGARIS
Yellow loosestrife. *An often invasive perennial with long-lasting flower* ● *spires through summer.*

VARIATIONS ON YELLOW

YELLOW IS AN EASY MIXER, shining happily alongside most other colours. With violet, its contrasting partner on the colour wheel, yellow is at its most vibrant; with close neighbours red and orange it makes the most melodious mix; so too with green. Elegant beside the tranquillity of blue, yellow gets from white its pure ethereal innocence. And although I have frequently heard said that yellow and pink have no place together in the garden, I look upon the two of them as well-matched, genial bedfellows.

ASCLEPIAS TUBEROSA
Butterfly weed. *A vigorous perennial that grows from a taproot. Large pods succeed the flowers.* •

HELIANTHUS ANNUUS
'TAIYO' Sunflower. *An erect, leafy annual of rapid growth reaching* • *1.2m (4ft).*

RELATED COLOUR SWATCH

A favourite composition of mine, bright orange, deep gold, and cream with glowing pink is a colour mix to be treasured. The first three are culled from the warm side of the colour wheel and make beautiful harmony. Reflecting their soft hues with its overtones of palest peach, pink (also a warm colour) adds interest to the group without the introduction of discordant notes.

CHELONE OBLIQUA Turtle-head. A perennial needing part shade and a moist soil, flowering in mid- or late summer until autumn.

ROSA 'MCGREDY'S YELLOW' Hybrid tea. A small shrub that bears fragrant double flowers continuously over a long period. Good for planting in groups.

HEIGHT OF COLOURFUL EXCITEMENT
White foxgloves, highlighted by dark green, form a soft backdrop to this gorgeous planting. Brilliant yellow daylily Hemerocallis lilio-asphodelus is splendid with bright green ligularia, intense orange Primula 'Inverewe', and ice-blue Myosotis caespitosa.

EMPHATIC DISCORD USED TO GOOD EFFECT
The sumptuous, rich shades of bluish red gladiolus and deep lilac erysimum sit companionably together, while warm yellow heads of mullein interrupt their harmony with a wanton gleam. Here, the combination of plants has been cleverly chosen in somewhat jarring tones, so that a small proportion of yellow will spark and bring an even greater degree of verve to the surrounding colours.

◀ RESONANT BALANCE

An offbeat plantscape of cool with warm, where the violet-blues of agapanthus and bellflower Campanula stir up vibrations in a minor key against the related oranges and yellows. Without the contrast of blue and orange, the view would have less life.

SNUG OUTLOOK ▶

Golden Spanish broom meets bluish pink sidalcea in a confidently energetic colour mix. A backing of solid rich dark green is an ideal foil. Silver foliage and pale peach poppies that seem to float add light relief.

GLITTERING NEIGHBOURS ▼

Strong, bright yellow coreposis grows in a luminous pool by straggling drifts of vivid carmine campion flowers set atop slender silver stems. On drear days and in shade, their colours will still be jewel-like bright.

A PURPLE CONTRAST

PURPLE IS THE RICHEST and most opulent of hues. Since early times it has been the symbol of status, a colour of preference denoting rank and nobility. Opposite purple in the colour wheel, the range of yellows (brilliant stars of the spectrum) have a luminous strength of their own. When the two come together, fireworks fly. Such intense contrasts are stimulating at first, but best used in relatively small quantities. A great swath of *Euphorbia polychroma* and deep magenta cranesbill *Geranium psilostemon* (*see left*) could be too much of a good thing in a small garden.

RELATED COLOUR SWATCH

Warm and cooler purples mingle with deep and clear yellows in a startling scheme for a midsummer border. *Gladiolus* 'Golden Standard', at right, is coolly defiant against the light-absorbing quality of purple larkspur. Alstroemeria and statice, near left, are less violent in their reaction, and enjoy a more cordial relationship.

LIMONIUM
SINUATUM Statice.
*A perennial grown as
an annual, flowering
in summer and early
autumn. It has an
untidy habit.*

MUTUAL SATISFACTION
*Subdued purple heads of ornamental onion Allium christophii
and radiant Chrysanthemum segetum 'Golden Gem' with its
emerald foliage meet in a symbiosis of colour. The gold enlivens
the purple which in turn endows the gold with greater brilliance.*

FAIR CONTEST
Monkey musk Mimulus luteus *has snapdragon-like flowers of rich yellow matched for strength in the intense purple of catmint* Nepeta x faassenii. *In plantings of such bold colour contrast, textural variety helps to prevent an overwhelming effect.*

CONSOLIDA AMBIGUA IMPERIAL SERIES Giant larkspur. *A hardy annual. The long flower spikes can* • *reach 1.2m (4ft).*

GLADIOLUS 'GOLDEN STANDARD'. *A hybrid growing from a corm, with flowers from* • *midsummer to early autumn.*

ALSTROEMERIA LIGTU HYBRIDS Peruvian lily. *A tuberous hardy perennial* • *that dislikes disturbance.*

REGAL MAJESTY

THE COLOURS OF POMP and splendour are wonderfully represented in the plant world. The rich velvety reds and purples of roses, gladioli, and clematis; the scarlet of poppies and dahlias: with these colours that combine so well together, a mood of glorious majesty reigns in the garden. Plants with purple foliage, such as *Cotinus coggygria* 'Royal Purple', *Weigela florida* 'Foliis Purpureis', and *Lobelia* 'Cherry Ripe', will emphasize the effect and create a planting of true magnificence.

RELATED COLOUR SWATCH

This stately group of plants, ceremoniously arrayed in sumptuous shades of crimson, cerise, and purple-pink, flowers at the same time near summer's end, bringing rich late-season colour to rejuvenate the garden. The roses begin earlier and must be regularly dead-headed and given a feed of rose fertilizer once their first flush is finished to ensure good successive shows of flowers.

CELOSIA ARGENTEA 'PLUMOSA' Feather *or* Plume cockscomb. *An annual with flowers in late summer, good for a border or containers.*

THE IRREPRESSIBLE ALLURE OF RED
Scarlet oriental poppy Papaver orientalis *has surely one of the most potent reds of any flower. The delicate frilled petals, each with a dark maroon blotch at the base, are exhibited high above a rosette of green leaves and give way to silver-grey seed heads. Blue borage* Borago officinalis *is seen, just opening, in front.*

ROYAL FLUSH
Few sights could be more opulent than this superb pairing of dark purple clematis 'Maureen' twined among heavy stems of deep cerise scrambling rose 'Pink Perpétué'. Both offer a rich display in early to midsummer, and then again late in the season.

LIATRIS SPICATA
Gayfeather. A perennial that produces its densely clothed long flower spikes ● *in late summer.*

GLADIOLUS 'JO WAGENAAR'
Large-flowered hybrid. Has mid- to late summer flowers ● *with a velvet sheen.*

ROSA 'ROUNDELAY' Modern shrub. *Bears intensely perfumed flowers, which open flat, from early summer to* ● *autumn.*

◀ COURTLY GROUP
Large and glossy blue-green leaves add a special lustre to the vivid crimson many-petalled flowers of 'L.D. Braithwaite', *a new English rose. Cranesbill* Geranium psilostemon, *with its black-eyed, bright magenta flowers, and crimson campion* Lychnis coronaria *complete the picture.*

▼ VULNERABLE GLORY
In a similar royal vein, strong red cactus Dahlia 'Alvas Doris' *has orbs composed of slender pointy petals; purple* Verbena patagonica *makes a surrounding sea of colour and texture that is the perfect foil. Both have a passing splendour as neither will stand up to cold winter temperatures except when grown in the mildest places.*

▲ DIGNIFIED ESTATE
*A magical garden combines its coroneted
arbour with plants that seem as if chosen
for their regal colours. Among foliage of
lush green, lupins stand majestically tall.
Palest pink old-fashioned roses, opening
from deeper buds, take centre stage with
violet delphiniums and frame a stunning
vista through to an amphitheatre of trees.*

ROSY OUTLOOK ▶
*Royal rose 'Queen of Denmark', an old
garden alba that's easy to grow, bears an
abundance of its stately pink blooms in a
single longish flowering during the height
of summer. It forms a lovely background
here to Lychnis coronaria with its silver
stems wreathed in rose-crimson flowers.*

EXUBERANT SUMMER

A VOLUPTUOUS MIX of strong and vibrant colours is a thrilling sight in the garden. Glowing reds, yellows, and oranges encapsulate summer in their rich bold tones. Planted in generous groups to create a landscape of undulating hills and valleys, they brim with a mood of summer plenty, and sit well alongside the cooler purples, blues, and pinks that give relief from too strident a view. This is the sort of planting that sets one's senses a-tingling, and in sunny heat radiates with the sheer joy of colour.

LYSIMACHIA VULGARIS
Yellow loosestrife. A long-flowering, clump-forming perennial that can be invasive.

RELATED COLOUR SWATCH

When colours of great intensity abound, greens play a major part. They make reds, oranges, and bright pinks leap forward, and take cool colours, in particular blue, into the background. Shades of gold- and lime-green, as in my bells of Ireland *Molucella laevis* at right, bring most colours vitality. Silver-grey or bronze set colours into hazy retreat, so work much better with soft hues.

HEART-WARMING REFRAIN
Mounding orange pot marigolds, lit up by feverfew Tanacetum parthenium 'Aureum' with its white daisy flowers and radiant emerald-green foliage, join a rousing chorus in this long border with purple and yellow pansies, red fuchsias, and copper roses.

JOYFUL ABSTRACT
Marvellous painterly effects are achieved with various hummock-forming plants placed in blocks of brilliant solid colour. In front at left, rose-pink and crimson pelargoniums merge into purple-blue Convolvulus mauritanicus. Scarlet poppies and vermilion valerian resound behind against drifts of perennial wallflower Erysimum 'Orange Flame'.

ROSA 'EDEN ROSE'
Hybrid tea. *A deciduous shrub with a profusion of scented flowers from early* ● *summer to autumn.*

AGERATUM HOUSTONIANUM
'PINKIE' Floss flower.
● *Midsummer annual.*

MOLUCELLA LAEVIS
Bells of Ireland. *An annual. Its lime-green calyces surround tiny scented white flowers.*

CALENDULA OFFICINALIS
Pot marigold. *A freely self-seeding annual with* ● *a pungent, tangy aroma.*

LUSH PARADISE ▶

Acting as foils to the purplish pink daisy flowers of Senecio pulcher, Euonymus japonicus *'Ovatus Aureus', burnt-rose* Leucothöe *'Flamingo', and* Phormium tenax *'Variegatum' (New Zealand flax) combine in a mix of subtropical flavour.*

◀ DARING DISPLAY

A planting of strawflower Helichrysum bracteatum *has a graphic simplicity. It's the inclusion of pink among the sunshine yellows, oranges, and reds that lifts it to the height of extraordinary flamboyance.*

▼ WHITE HEAT

Terraced chrysanthemums in white, ice-pink, and primrose-yellow present a cool contrast to extravagant gold and orange red-hot pokers Kniphofia, *intermingled with the rich cerise of watsonia in front.*

BRIGHT RED DAZZLERS

BOLD AND SASSY, red is the most forward of colours. Placed with green, the colour that lies directly opposite it in the colour wheel, it's even more so: it absolutely leaps out at you, almost with a life of its own. I enjoy red most of all used this way. Even if the combination is small scale, for instance plants in a container or a red climber festooned among the luxuriant green foliage of a tree, the effect always elicits an excited response. The strongest impact comes when shades of brilliant red veering somewhat toward orange rather than pink are set against dark glossy greens that resonate with their intensity.

IMPATIENS WALLERIANA BLITZ SERIES Busy Lizzie. *A large-flowered annual from early summer to first frost.*

RELATED COLOUR SWATCH

This unsophisticated grouping that combines just two different plants is an ideal choice for a container in a semi-shaded or even shaded position, instilling a note of vibrancy into a sombre view. Both the fast-growing busy Lizzie (*far left*) and begonia will give a wonderful spectacle of strong colour contrast from early summer through to autumn. Scented tobacco plant *Nicotiana alata* and fuchsias would also make suitable additions.

BEGONIA 'CLIPS'. *Excellent for growing in containers, a typical B. x tuberhybrida (Multiflora group) that bears large double flowers on sturdy stems.*

LIBERTY BELLE
Brilliant scarlet flame flower Tropaeolum speciosum *clambers up into a dark green yew hedge. It's a real dazzler that needs to be planted about 28cm (10in) deep in a rich acid soil with roots in shade and flowers in sun. Once established, it's unstoppable.*

SEASIDE FROLICS
Give red valerian Centranthus ruber *a brick or rocky crevice to grow in (especially near the sea) and it will romp away with abandon. Not so intense a red as some, its massed flower spires still create a fiery show against a strong background of greenery.*

CONSTANT GREEN

GARDEN SALAD GREENS

ELEGANT, COOL, AND SERENE, green is a constant factor in the garden, particularly in summer months, imparting a sense of great wellbeing. It can be there as a lush leafy background to show off the myriad colours of flowers; and it can be there in its own right. A host of plants are used and valued for their leaves alone: unlikely contenders as the lettuce and cabbage (*left*) may seem, they too can play a decorative role. Use foliage in all its forms for each separate effect. Golden green gives life to colours; rich green intensifies them; copper and purple make red, blue, and yellow withdrawn, even muddied.

RELATED COLOUR SWATCH

Greens come together in an intriguing mix to create a gentle muted mood. Bronze, silver, subtle plum-tinged grey, and white-with-green tempt the eye with visions of healing repose. Mingled with evergreens in a sunny mixed foliage border, where flowers take only a minor part, such greens will look beautiful through the year.

UNDER SPREADING LEAFY TREES
Bright golden false acacia Robinia pseudoacacia *'Frisia' stand forward against the rich green backdrop of trees and the band of dark yew hedging below. They hold their fresh spring-like colour to late autumn, and are one of the last trees to lose their leaves.*

AROUND A MOSSY PEBBLE-EDGED POOL
A shady woodland verge is a wonderful place for a grouping of special foliage plants. Bright lemon-splashed variegated hostas, lime-green shuttlecock fern Matteuccia struthiopteris, and cut-leaved sinuous Japanese aralia Fatsia japonica recede into the cool glaucous blue of Hosta sieboldiana.

SENECIO 'SUNSHINE'. *A moundy evergreen shrub bearing small yellow flowers in summer. The youngest leaves are the most silver.*

COTINUS COGGYGRIA 'NOTCUTT'S VARIETY' Smoke tree. *Mature dull green foliage is set off by tender young leaves that open red-bronze.*

SALVIA OFFICINALIS 'PURPURASCENS' Purple sage. *The textured purple-tinged new leaves are held on violet stems.*

EUPHORBIA MARGINATA Snow-in-summer. *An annual with showy white bracts surrounding each set of tiny flowers.*

◀ ENCHANTED KINGDOM
A composition in greens is ideally sited at the edge of a feathery canopy of conifers on a hillside. Astonishing blue-green and bright green join in a meditative world of hostas, ferns, grasses, and rhododendron.

SUBSTANTIAL ILLUSION ▶
Variegated Russian comfrey Symphytum x uplandicum 'Variegatum' has creamy-margined leaves throughout summer that seem almost like dappled sunshine against their backdrop of golden American elder.

▼ COOL PROSPECT
Sunbeams dance and cast their spell over a shady glade of ferns, irises, grasses, and candelabra primroses. Coppery green flax Phormium tenax 'Purpureum' gives the planting an upswing of dramatic interest.

PEACEFUL PASTELS

LAVATERA 'BARNSLEY'

MY FIRST SIGHT of an early summer alpine meadow was in northern Italy. Its beauty was breathtaking, an impressionistic dream made up of mostly pastel colours. Bringing this vision into the garden is very simple, for these colours, which are full of light, take to each other like rosy-flushed peaches mixed with thick rich cream. Lemon and apricot; confections in soft rose (the mallow at left) and other quiet pinks; pale lilac, silver-blue, and of course not forgetting white: all or any of them mingle with ease in a picture of great loveliness and unerring quality.

RELATED COLOUR SWATCH

A soothing scheme where the lilies' stamens have the strongest colour, a bright orange reverberating against sumptuous hollyhock blooms in an apricot shade that looks amazing beside the ice-pink lily petals. Here too are lilac everlasting statice (easy to grow and ideal for drying), white loosestrife spikes, and greeny gold dill.

LYSIMACHIA CLETHROIDES
Loosestrife. *A perennial that prefers a not too dry site.*

BY WINDING WAYS
Pinks, yellows, and white spill out over a path: their soft colours sit well with the texture of brick. Daisy Erigeron mucronatum at left goes on for months and the massed honey-gold flowers of meadow foam Limnanthes douglassii are seldom far behind.

LIMONIUM SINUATUM
Statice. *A bushy perennial grown as an annual. Seed can be bought for many single colours.*

WATERSIDE CONTEMPLATION
*Beside a dark pond, Hosta sieboldiana flourishes
its magnificently corrugated silver-blue leaves – as
yet unmolested by snails. In company with softest
pink and white candelabra Primula pulverulenta
'Bartley', other deeper pink primulas, and the still
water, it makes a gentle and reflective planting.*

ANETHUM GRAVEOLENS Dill.
*A self-seeding annual. Every
part of the plant has a buttery,
aromatic fragrance.*

ALCEA ROSEA
'CHATER'S DOUBLE'
Hollyhock. *A rust-free
biennial selection in
varied colours.*

LILIUM 'LE REVE' Lily.
*A bulb producing
flowers with the
most heavenly
sweet scent.*

WILD MEADOW LAND ▶

The soft contours of clipped golden yews stand as focal points in a view where the colours of columbines play on each other like gentle breezes. Above, the clear pink late-season blossom of a Judas tree rises toward creamy variegated foliage greens.

◀ EXOTIC PAIR

Reminiscent of a Mediterranean hillside, sharp yellow Foeniculum vulgare *joins the violet hues of* Verbena patagonica. *When the sun is at its midsummer peak, stronger pastels will still shine against it.*

▼ SUBTLE SUGGESTION

A mix of plants that has an easy natural charm. Pale with deeper pink Dianthus 'Doris' echo the tones of daisy Erigeron mucronatum *and catmint Nepeta 'Six Hills Giant' adds a dusky lavender glow.*

Autumn

❋

Brilliantly tinted foliage dances along
outstretched branches of Japanese
maples, and is made all the more
gorgeous by glimpses of contrasting
green in the grass beneath and rough
lichened bark of adjoining trees.

PALETTE FOR AUTUMN

A month or so before the end of summer a new mood stirs, heralding autumn. Nights are cooler, heavy dews collect, and the whole colour palette begins to change. As autumn gathers pace, sultry tones take over. Oranges, reds, and golden yellows triumph in chrysanthemums and dahlias. Asters amaze in marvellous purples, blues, and mellow pinks. Then flowers give way to glowing berries and the glorious spectacle of autumn leaves.

EVENTIDE IN THE RHYTHM OF LIFE
Decay is more apparent in wild parts of the garden. Leaves turn colour and fall, providing nourishment for next year's growth: green is overtaken by gold, and rust, and brown. Mists drift in these mornings, especially where water is. As the sun breaks through, the garden basks again in warm and honeyed light.

- YELLOW *reflects the sinking of the sun and a remembered summer warmth in many daisy flowers. Later, foliage adds its mellow tones.*

- PINK *reigns strongly at this time of year in dusky hues, and veers toward the soft violets and blues of the colour wheel. Their beauty is seen in many sedums, Michaelmas daisies, and hydrangeas.*

- ORANGE *fits autumn to perfection: it is as if the myriad patchwork of summer colour has been heaped on a fire in a burst of flame at the end of the year.*

- RED *is rich, deep, like Burgundy wine. As chrysanthemums and dahlias glow, the quickening leaves of sumachs, acers, and prunus burn darkly before they fall.*

- SCARLET *puts on a glorious bright parade in the fruits of many plants. Guelder rose, pyracantha, oriental bittersweet, and holly have some of the best.*

INCANDESCENT FIRE

SCARLET, VERMILION, RUBY, carmine, crimson: all these violent shades are centred around vivacious red. Autumn offers a plethora of incandescent border wonders in various forms of dahlia, kaffir lily, nerine, and crocosmia, besides a wealth of berries and other fruits. Their range of tone is extremely forward – even brash – and all leap out of their beds in colours that astound us with their brightness and sheer audacity. Most potent against green, they also clamour with a raucous voice when intermixed with purples and blues.

ASTER NOVI-BELGII 'EVENTIDE' Michaelmas daisy. *A pretty, favourite perennial prone to insect and mildew attack.*

NERINE SARNIENSIS VAR. *CORUSCA* Guernsey lily. *A bulb. Grow outdoors only in mild places.*

RELATED COLOUR SWATCH

If pure primary red is one of the most forward colours of the wheel, scarlet and reds that lean toward orange are surely the most fiery. Their jack-in-a-box capacity to spring out of the landscape can almost overwhelm, yet their lively tribute to the joy of summer's plenty is an apt prelude to the quieter, less active seasons. This stunning group teams the crystalline flowers of nerine with cotoneaster and light-as-air Michaelmas daisies.

COTONEASTER HUPEHENSIS. A deciduous shrub of arching habit with the advantage of yellow autumn colour and • *profuse fruit clusters.*

DESIGNED TO SHOCK
Flame-red and crimson dahlias with tropical-leaved cannas and purple verbena make whacky companions. Dahlias 'Bishop of Llandaff' and 'Sure Thing' are about as spirited as any flowers can be, and look even more so in association with the verbena.

RACING THROUGH THE SEASONS
Crocosmia quickly forms clumps of its late summer to autumn flower spires in colours ranging from orange to gold and yellow to blazing red. Purple Verbena patagonica jumps up in front.

THE SETTING SUN

SYMPATHETIC MARRIAGE

HARMONY SITS at the heart of autumn in the tawny rusts, rich dark reds, earth-browns, and radiant burned orange that share the hot part of the colour wheel. Their closely allied warmth reflects the tones of bonfires and a setting sun, and in the garden they lend a melodious yet fading heat to the year's colour parade. Beside autumnal favourites, such as the floribunda roses seen with bronze canna foliage at left, the final glory of summer goes on in begonias, fuchsias, pelargoniums, and nasturtiums.

DAHLIA Water-lily type. A tuberous perennial, one of the numerous border hybrids. It will flower until first frost.

RELATED COLOUR SWATCH

A dusky group illumined by the candied sweet orange of red-hot pokers will look especially wondrous as the sun dips to the horizon. Blending chocolate and gold, russet and blood-red, it takes us on a journey from the crackling midst of the bonfire to its dark, smoky outer edges that barely catch the dwindling rays of daylight.

COMPOSITION FOR ONE VOICE
All the harmonious colours of the season are captured in a single plant. Shifting from glowing scarlet through musky orange to old gold, the petals of sneezeweed Helenium autumnale *are set off by large globular pompons of hazy ochre and toasted brown.*

ENDURING MELODY
Chrysanthemums have a honey tang that echoes their embered hues. These reflexed and pompon cultivars are covered in flower for weeks from late summer until cold weather sets in. Underplanted below, nasturtiums ping against their vivid leaves.

KNIPHOFIA TRIANGULARIS
Red-hot poker. *A perennial with small flower spikes borne on wiry stems.*

LEYCESTERIA FORMOSA
Himalayan honeysuckle. *A deciduous shrub. The white flowers with purple-red bracts produce purplish autumn fruits.*

CHRYSANTHEMUM *Non-disbudded type. An early autumn perennial bearing sprays of flowers that are ideal for cutting.*

RADIANT GOLD

NOT ONLY CAN autumn's touch turn many plants to gleaming gold: many autumn plants bear golden flowers and fruits besides. From red-gold to pale gold and brilliant yellow-golds, this is the colour that fits the mellow feel of autumn; and it's important to make the most of each season's particular gifts so that beds and borders (containers too) can shine in every month. Autumn flowers with golden-leaved shrubs will look marvellously apt now and still appeal for the rest of the year.

CHRYSANTHEMUM 'WENDY' Spray florists'. *A half-hardy perennial with reflexed flowers in early autumn.*

RELATED COLOUR SWATCH

Plants whose flowers span the slow change of summer to autumn are specially valuable in the garden. There are even some indefatigable annuals such as begonias, antirrhinums, and tagetes, all with forms in gold, that start with an early summer flush and go on to the first frost. The strawflowers and chrysanthemums here will bloom from late summer right through autumn, while the young eucalyptus foliage is often tinged with gold.

BEFORE THE FALL
Stag's horn sumach Rhus hirta, *pictured in its form 'Laciniata' which makes a small tree, has leaves that expire in a wonderful burst of colour through rich gold and oranges to striking scarlet. Hickory, beech, and sassafras also supply fine autumnal golds.*

STARRY TREASURE TROVE
The strong contrast of nearly black eyes highlights a generous clump of coneflower Rudbeckia hirta 'Marmalade', with their gilded yellow petals. For a particularly prolific autumn show, cut back and feed the plants after their first summer flowering.

CHRYSANTHEMUM 'YELLOW BREITNER' *Reflexed florists'. An early autumn perennial. Grow from rooted cuttings* • *planted in late spring.*

EUCALYPTUS TORQUATA Coral gum. *A slender, fairly hardy evergreen tree that will* • *reach 8m (25ft).*

HELICHRYSUM BRACTEATUM Strawflower. *A branching annual form flowering from* • *summer to early autumn.*

FLICKERING EMBERS

I AM ALWAYS HAPPY to return to one of my favourite colour combinations. Pink and orange make such glad companions, and are especially cheerful with an injection of pale or golden green. As the season moves on and the garden is readied for winter, it is good to have planned for a farewell vision of animated colour. Dahlias, nerines, belladonna lilies, and later-flowering hebes contribute plenty of pinks and oranges to the season's palette. Many roses, too, have flowers and fruits in wondrous shades of these two colours.

AMARYLLIS BELLADONNA Belladonna lily. *A bulb producing its flower stems in early autumn after the leaves die down.* •

RELATED COLOUR SWATCH

Rugosa rose hips the size and colour of tiny tomatoes, fragile papery ribbed lanterns of *Physalis alkekengi*, and luminous nerines provide elements of brilliant orange in this group for an autumn border. The sugar-pink of sweetly fragrant belladonna lilies and rouged carmine of *Hebe* 'La Séduisante' impart a glow of soft warmth.

ROSA RUGOSA • 'SCABROSA' Species hybrid. *A dense shrub. The large fruits follow a long succession of richly scented, cupped, single pink flowers.*

SPLENDID LATE ARRAY
A deep border can be every bit as delightful in autumn as it is in summer. Fringing and overflowing the edge of lawn, crocosmia, amaranth, penstemon, and yarrow; rudbeckia, mallow, dahlia, and rose are alive with form, texture, and joyful play of colour.

FIREBRAND DISPLAY
Red-hot pokers stand like gleaming torches against a bronze-purple smoke tree and deep pink Joe Pye weed. Pale lemon-green mullein and goat's beard emphasize the zingy clash of orange with pink.

HEBE 'LA SEDUISANTE'.
A slightly tender evergreen shrub for a sheltered site, with dense flower spikes
• throughout autumn.

NERINE 'CORUSCA MAJOR'.
A half-hardy bulb. Plant in the shelter of a warm sunny wall.
• Protect from winter chill.

PHYSALIS ALKEKENGI
Chinese lantern. A hardy perennial that needs to be controlled. Edible fruits are
• inside the lantern calyces.

Winter

With the landscape of colour at its most sombre, the pure clean beauty of other detail comes into its own in the outlines of trees, thrusting sappy young shoots, rich evergreens, and flowers that shine like tiny jewels.

PALETTE FOR WINTER

Dominated by the brown of soil, the grey of bark, persistent foliage greens, and a sprinkling of berries, winter may seem short on colour interest. Yet the garden still has magic. The sharply defined bones of trees and shrubs laid bare produce intricate patterns. Evergreen forms abound in gold, copper, and silver-blue. Camellias and other shrubs grace the view with winter flowers, while crocus and snowdrop speak sweet messages of spring.

A STUDY IN MINIMALISM
Crisp dried-up hortensia hydrangea heads have a spare beauty, intensified by flooding winter-white light. The plumed branches, with once-colourful bracts now coated in frost, are reduced to shades of frothy cappuccino. In the foreground at right, a robin redbreast broods plumply atop a small evergreen rhododendron.

● GREY-BROWN *is a bold feature of winter's scene in the form of bare earth, bark, and catkins. Dead leaves littering the ground or held on hedging plants like hornbeam and beech add interesting texture.*

● WHITE *has the dominant note in flowers. Viburnums and heathers (precious spots of light) gleam bright against sombre foliage, and survive the chill of winter thanks to their energy-conserving size.*

● COPPER, *shading to red through bronze, appears in evergreen leaves and forms of pittosporum, leucothöe, photinia, phormium, and cordyline. Purple varieties extend this colour range.*

● SILVER *and biting tones of iron-green echo the cold patinas of winter. As with white, they give a brilliant sheen to drear landscapes. Many conifers, santolinas, and artemisias have useful silver-grey winter foliage.*

● RICH EVERGREENS *have a special value at this time, providing definition for the garden and a suggestion of spring's freshness. Berries are a bonus on small trees and shrubs including holly, skimmia, and firethorn.*

WINTER CHEER

FEMALE *SKIMMIA JAPONICA*

FACED WITH THE AUSTERITY of the seasonal landscape, red and green meet in opposing colours whose contrast is even more intense than at other times of year. Berries will be the surest source of winter reds (if birds have not taken them all) but when planning for them, remember that some plants need a male and a female to produce their fruits – the skimmia (*left*) is one such. Winter shoots can make strong features too. Willow *Salix alba* 'Britzensis' has a tracery of scarlet young stems that look particularly beautiful near water.

RELATED COLOUR SWATCH

This vigorous quartet of plants has cheer sufficient to brighten the greyest outlook. A glowing collection of stout-hearted spiky holly, dogwood stems, fruiting ivy, and cotoneaster provides an exciting variety of colour and texture in its glossy and ribbed evergreen foliage, mahogany winter shoots, and clustered scarlet berries. No less showy, the green ivy fruit ripens to coal-black.

SKELETON FRAMEWORK
'Westonbirt' is a selection of red-barked dogwood Cornus alba, here with its whippy new shoots striking out boldly from ground bedded in snow. C. stolonifera 'Flaviramea' has lemon shoots in winter. Prune both low in spring to encourage young growth.

ILEX AQUIFOLIUM
Common holly.
A slow-growing evergreen tree that has many different forms. The fruit is particularly profuse after dry summers.

NATURAL WONDERS
When the garden lacks colour, other parts of the scene can fill the gap. The hard-edged blue of a winter sky is nature's own surprise. It makes an incredible backdrop to the brilliant red berries of guelder rose Viburnum opulus that succeed its lace-cap white flowers and tinted autumn foliage.

CORNUS ALBA *Red-barked dogwood. A deciduous shrub with red new growth in winter. C. alba 'Elegantissima' has variegated summer foliage.* •

COTONEASTER 'CORNUBIA'. *A semi-evergreen shrub of arching habit. Clusters of white flowers in early summer are followed by copious quantities of berries.* •

HEDERA HELIX *Common English ivy. A self-clinging evergreen climber with berries only on older tree-like growth.* •

ARCHITECTURAL GREEN

IT IS IN WINTER that greens come with renewed vigour into their own, for this is the time of year when much of the competition is gone from the garden. Bold shapes and textures (not forgetting those of branches and bark) impress their definition on areas that lack colour, replacing it with structural interest. Box and yew clip into perfect topiaries; privet makes a neat hedge. And if colour is wanted, many trees have forms with gold, blue, or silver foliage.

LARIX DECIDUA European larch. A deciduous conifer that has light green foliage, golden in autumn. It grows fast, reaching as much as 30m (100ft). •

RELATED COLOUR SWATCH

Striking leaves and twigs in varied shades of green, as well as excitingly different textures, produce splendid effects. In the garden (which may languish in winter) they make noteworthy features that transform it from summer's down-at-heel relation into something really special. Here, deciduous larch twigs covered in lichen and moss join New Zealand flax, crinkly pittosporum, silver-backed elaeagnus, and sprays of golden cypress.

ORNAMENTAL FROSTING
Mahonias – in particular the taller ones – have dramatic leaves, held like outstretched palm fronds on plants that make shrubs or small trees. Slightly tender M. lomarifolia (my favourite) and the hardier hybrid M. x media 'Charity' have scented flowers.

CORSICAN BEAUTY
Lenten rose Helleborus lividus *subsp.* corsicus
often produces its pale greenish white flowers in
late winter, with successive showings until spring.
Its spine-toothed leaves are evergreen. For subtle
colour, choose H. x sternii 'Blackthorn' with its
silver-pink foliage and green flowers flushed pink.

ELAEAGNUS x EBBINGEI.
An evergreen shrub. The
tiny tubular white autumn
flowers have a strong
gardenia scent. •

PHORMIUM TENAX New
Zealand flax. An evergreen
perennial variegated in gold,
bronze, silver, cream, and
purple. •

PITTOSPORUM TENUIFOLIUM
'VARIEGATUM'. A large shrub
or small evergreen tree that
thrives by the sea. •

CUPRESSUS MACROCARPA
'GOLDCREST' Monterey
cypress. A fast-growing
evergreen conifer with
• lemon-scented foliage.

VENERABLE MONUMENTS ▶

In its tree form or toped into shape, yew will live for hundreds of years: one of the most famous English topiary gardens can boast plants living in their fiftieth decade. When planning these strong, ornamental shapes, it's as well to remember that yew can put on about 25cm (10in) a year.

◀ COAT OF MANY COLOURS

Winter hues and patterns may need a bit of searching out, but are quite superb in their detail; and so it is with Leucothöe fontanesiana 'Rainbow'. The evergreen leaves, shown in their seasonal red dress, are further defined by a dusting of frost.

▲ NINE-DAYS WONDER

Silk-tassel bush Garrya elliptica bears magnificent catkins that hang on its branches like Christmas decorations from midwinter to spring. Careful siting is a must, for its dark green foliage can make it a dull feature at other times when the flowers are gone.

▲ YEAR-ROUND SPECTACLE

On cold winter days, box and mounding evergreen honeysuckle Lonicera nitida 'Baggeson's Gold' take on a blue-green frosted air. They're particularly good topiary subjects, as are privet and yew, and will look fantastic at every season – including winter.

MIDWINTER WHITE

SILKY CLEMATIS SEEDHEADS

THE COLOUR OF SNOW AND FROST seems particularly right for winter plantings and the mood of quiet watchfulness. When the weather is mild, white brings nostalgia, too, for the crisp beauty of hoarier days. The vagaries of regional climate will dictate the plants you choose. At this time of year, the absence of eye-engaging colour lends grasses and seedheads, such as those of clematis (*left*) a unique appeal. For flowers, Christmas roses are the earliest white, followed by snowdrops and – in milder areas – white quince and heather.

RELATED COLOUR SWATCH

This seasonal planting for a bed against the shelter of a wall will flower in mild midwinter spells through to spring. *Senecio* 'Sunshine' has leaves whose soft felted undersides are echoed in cream-white Christmas rose *Helleborus niger* and heather, opening from pink buds. Flowering quince adds blossoms of spare, pure white.

AIRS AND GRACES
Pampas grass Cortaderia selloana *needs room for such drama: plants soon form a massive clump, and are often invasive. The graceful ivory flower plumes can reach a height of 3m (10ft) or more together with the leaves, but should be removed in spring.*

SENECIO 'SUNSHINE'. *A bushy evergreen shrub with coarse yellow flowers, best kept as a foliage plant.*

LATE WINTER GREETS SPRING
The first snowdrops are a welcome sight, for they seem to say that spring is not too far away. Of the many sorts, I think the simple common snowdrop Galanthus nivalis *most lovely with its grey-green leaves, especially carpeting the edge of woodland.*

CHAENOMELES SPECIOSA
'NIVALIS' Flowering quince. *A deciduous, thorny shrub, excellent for training against a sheltered sunny wall.*

HELLEBORUS NIGER
Christmas rose. *A clump-forming evergreen perennial. In sheltered sites, its usually winter to spring flowers appear in early winter.*

ERICA ERIGENA
Heather. *A tall and frost-hardy evergreen shrub with flowers from early winter until late spring.*

PROMISE OF SPRING

WITH THE INEXORABLE movement of life, winter will start to give way to spring and colour creep into the garden again. In the meantime, some plants defy the bleak mood that can slide over midwinter, and produce flowers and foliage to make you feel that spring has already come. The scent of young growth fills the air in a burst of vitality, and hearts skip a beat. Yellows and golds, rich pinks, cream, and fresh foliage greens capture the colours of early spring and act like rays of sunshine on a wintry scene.

LEUCOTHÖE FONTANESIANA 'RAINBOW'. An arching evergreen shrub. The bronze young leaves mature to dark green, at first splashed pink turning to cream.

RELATED COLOUR SWATCH

A combination of pink, yellow, and white, gentle and heartening against the supple bronze leucothöe leaves and dark evergreen camellia, would be hard to surpass on a winter's day. Scent is a bonus that intensifies the ebullient mood, for these white viburnum and yellow witch hazel flowers smell delicious. Plant the camellia out of morning sun so that its flowers remain spotless.

GOOD OMEN
Winter aconite Eranthis hyemalis can be really early to bloom. It throws up its single clear spring-yellow buttercup-like flowers, with their ruff of green leaves, from tubers, even through snow and ice. A little fussy, it likes dappled shade and rich moist soil.

144

MESSAGE FROM AN EXOTIC LAND
The fat buds of Japanese apricot Prunus mume
'Beni-shidare' can appear as soon as late winter,
and in warm periods they burst open to flood the
garden with vivid colour. 'Pendula' is a weeping
form, also with early flowers but of a paler pink.

VIBURNUM x BODNANTENSE.
An upright deciduous shrub.
Its vanilla-scented flowers
open in mild spells from late
• autumn until early spring.

CAMELLIA JAPONICA
'TAKASAGO'. *An evergreen*
shrub – a Higo Japonica
cultivar whose flowers
are distinguished by
their large golden
• yellow bosses.

HAMAMELIS MOLLIS 'PALLIDA' *Chinese*
witch hazel. A large deciduous shrub with
yellow autumn foliage. The winter flowers
have an intensely sweet yet delicate scent. •

SEASONAL PLANT IDEAS

To help you select plants by colour in each of the four seasons, I've put together a list (*pages 146 to 153*) that contains some unusual kinds as well as familiar and favourite ones. It is intended simply to spark off your own ideas.

The descriptions provide notes on culture and site, e.g. rich soil, full sun; flowering time; and colour range of flowers (in few cases leaves or fruit). Generally, all are best in a well-drained soil, and will flower throughout their season.

❧ SPRING ❧

TREES, SHRUBS, & CLIMBERS

Acacia MIMOSA, WATTLE.
Fast-growing evergreen trees. Sun, frost protection. Early spring. *Bright yellow.*

Aesculus hippocastanum HORSE CHESTNUT.
Large deciduous tree. Sun or part shade. Late spring. *Creamy white with dark pink to red blotches.*

Akebia quinata.
Deciduous or semi-evergreen climber. Rich soil, sun or part shade. Late spring. *Dark purple.*

Amelanchier SNOWY MESPILUS.
Small deciduous trees. Sun or part shade. Mid-spring. *White.*

Arbutus STRAWBERRY TREE.
Small to large evergreen trees with reddish bark. Lime-free soil, sun with shelter. Mid-spring. (Red autumn fruit.) *White.*

Azara.
Evergreen shrubs or small trees. Rich soil, sun or part shade with wall shelter. *Bright yellow.*

Berberis BARBERRY.
Deciduous free-flowering shrubs. Sun. (Coloured autumn fruit.) *Yellow, orange, apricot, red.*

Camellia.
Evergreen shrubs or small trees. Acid soil, part shade with shelter. Winter to spring. *Yellow, red, pink, white.*

CORNUS FLORIDA 'CHEROKEE CHIEF'

Chaenomeles FLOWERING QUINCE.
Deciduous shrubs. Sun or part shade. *Orange, red, pink, white.*

Choisya ternata MEXICAN ORANGE BLOSSOM.
Evergreen, aromatic shrub. Rich soil, sun or part shade. Flowers occasionally throughout year. *White.*

Clematis montana.
Deciduous climber to 10m/30ft. Alkaline soil, base in shade, shoots in sun. Profuse 4-petalled flowers. *Pink, white.*

Cornus florida FLOWERING DOGWOOD.
Large deciduous shrub with showy bracts. Rich soil, Sun. *Pink, white.*

Cytisus canariensis BROOM.
Large evergreen shrub. Sun with shelter. Profuse flowers late winter to midsummer. *Yellow.*

Daphne.
Evergreen & deciduous shrubs, most with scented flowers. Sun with shelter (but *D. laureola* will tolerate deep shade). *Pink, white.*

Erica cinerea, E. x darlyensis HEATHER.
Evergreen sub-shrubs. Moist acid soil, sun. Winter through spring. *Pink, purple, white.*

Euphorbia characias, E. mellifera, E. myrsinites, E. polychroma, E. rigida.
Evergreen & deciduous sub-shrubs (& perennials) with showy bracteated flowerheads. Sun. Bracts *Gold, lime-green.*

Forsythia.
Large deciduous shrubs. Sun or part shade. Mid-spring before leaves emerge. *Bright yellow.*

Kerria JEW'S MALLOW.
Large free-flowering deciduous shrubs with single or double flowers. Sun or part shade. Mid-spring. *Yellow.*

Magnolia denudata, M. salicifolia, M. x soulangeana, M. stellata.
Deciduous large shrubs or small trees. Rich soil (better lime free), sun with shelter from strong cold winds. Tulip-shaped flowers are produced before leaves unfold. *Pink, purple, white.*

Malus CRABAPPLE.
Small or medium-sized deciduous trees. Rich soil, full sun. Flowers at the same time as leaves unfold. *Pink, white.*

Osmanthus.
Medium to large evergreen shrubs. Full sun with shelter from cold wind. Vanilla-scented flowers late spring. *White.*

Pieris.
Large evergreen shrubs. Moist acid soil, bright site with shade. Varieties of *P. formosa* have coral, salmon, & red new leaves at same time as flowers. *White.*

Prunus CHERRY.
Small to medium deciduous trees. Full sun. Single or double flowers mid- to late spring. (*P. sargentii* has rich autumn colour.) *Pink, white.*

Rhododendron (includes **Azalea**).
Evergreen & deciduous small to large shrubs. Moist acid soil, part shade with some shelter. Bears trumpet-shaped flowers in heads, mostly late spring. *Yellow, orange, red, pink, purple, white.*

PIERIS JAPONICA 'FLAMINGO'

Ribes FLOWERING CURRANT.
Medium-sized to large deciduous shrubs. Sun or part shade. Flowers borne in racemes early spring. *Yellow, red, pink, white.*

Sophora tetraptera KOWHAI.
Large half-hardy deciduous shrub or small tree. Rich soil, full sun against a wall for shelter. Waxy pea-like flowers mid-spring. *Golden yellow.*

Spiraea x arguta,
S. thunbergii BRIDAL WREATH.
Medium-sized deciduous shrubs. Wreaths of tiny flowers mid- to late spring. *White.*

Staphylea BLADDER NUT.
Large deciduous shrubs or small trees with vanilla-scented flowers. Moist rich soil, full sun. Late spring. *Pink, white.*

Syringa. LILAC.
Medium to large deciduous shrubs or small trees. Rich soil, sun or part shade. Fragrant flowers after 2–3 years' established growth. *Pink, purple, lilac, white, cream.*

Viburnum plicatum
JAPANESE SNOWBALL.
Large deciduous shrub. Moist rich soil, full sun. Flowerheads on lateral shoots. *Pink, white.*

ANNUALS & BIENNIALS

Bellis DAISY.
Grow as biennials. Rich soil, sun or part shade. Regular dead-heading provides single & double flowers early spring through to summer. *Red, pink, white.*

Erysimum WALLFLOWER.
Grow as biennials. Any but not acid soil, sun. Highly scented flowers produced in spikes late spring. *Yellow, orange, red, pink, purple, cream.*

Lunaria HONESTY.
Grow as biennials. Part shade. Sweetly fragrant flowers mid- to late spring (silver seedpods autumn). *Pink, purple, white.*

Myosotis FORGET-ME-NOT.
Grow as biennials. Moist soil, sun or shade. Most varieties with pure blue flowers mid-spring to early summer. *Range of blues.*

ERYSIMUM 'JOHN CODRINGTON'

Senecio x hybridus CINERARIA.
Half-hardy biennials. Soil well-drained but not dry, sun or part shade. Flowerheads mid-spring to early summer. *Orange, red, pink, violet, purple, blue, white.*

PERENNIALS & BULBS

Allium ORNAMENTAL ONION.
Small to large bulbs. The narrow strap-like leaves have an onion smell when crushed. Sun. Plant out in autumn. Flowers, borne in umbels, appear late spring to early summer depending on species. *Yellow, pink, purple, blue, white.*

Bergenia.
Herbaceous perennials. Sun or part shade. Leaves large, leathery, evergreen. Flowers in heads late winter, spring, & early summer. *Rust, pink, purple, white.*

Chionodoxa
GLORY OF THE SNOW.
Small clump-forming bulbs. Sun. Some have flowers of purest blue. Early spring. *Pink, blue, white.*

Crocus.
Small-growing bulbs, naturalizing in grass. Sun or part shade. Early spring (or autumn) depending on species. *Yellow, orange, purple, blue, white.*

Erythronium.
Grows from a tuber resembling a dog's tooth. Rich soil, part shade or shade. Delicate bell-shaped flowers above rosettes of leaves (often spotted) late spring. *Yellow, pink, purple, cream.*

Fritillaria imperialis
CROWN IMPERIAL FRITILLARY.
Large bulb. Bright part shade. Beautiful flowers but with an unpleasant rodent smell. *Yellow, orange, red.*

Fritillaria meleagris
SNAKE SKIN FRITILLARY.
Medium bulb that will naturalize well in grass. Bright part shade. *Brown, purple, green, white.*

Galanthus SNOWDROP.
Small-growing bulbs. Sun or part shade. Bell-shaped flowers, held on delicate stems, early spring. *White (most with green markings).*

Hyacinthoides non-scriptus
ENGLISH BLUEBELL.
Large bulb. Will naturalize in and carpet light woodland. Moist soil, part shade. Lightly scented bell flowers are borne in short spires. *Pink, intense blue, white.*

Hyacinthus HYACINTH.
Small to medium-growing bulbs. Sun or part shade. Intensely perfumed flower spikes mid- to late spring. *Salmon, red, pink, purple, blue, white.*

Leucojum SNOWFLAKE.
Low to medium bulbs. Well-drained but not dry soil, sun or part shade. *L. vernum* (small) & *L. aestivum* (medium) have snowdrop-like flowers with green markings. (Some species flower autumn.) *White.*

Muscari GRAPE HYACINTH.
Low clump-forming bulbs. Sun or bright shade. Strap-shaped leaves. Flowers have sweet butter scent. *Range of blues, white.*

HYACINTHUS 'JAN BOS'

Narcissus DAFFODIL.
Large group of low- & medium-growing bulbs, many of which will naturalize well in grass. Sun or part shade. *Yellow, orange, pink, cream, white.*

Polygonatum
SOLOMON'S SEAL.
Elegant & demure perennials. Rich soil, part shade. Bell-shaped flowers are borne along leafy stems. *White edged with green.*

Primula vulgaris
POLYANTHUS & PRIMROSE.
Low clump-forming perennials. Moist soil, sun or part shade. *Primrose-yellow, gold, orange, red, pink, purple, violet, white.*

Pulmonaria LUNGWORT.
Low-growing perennials. Sun or part shade. *Red, pink, blue, white.*

TULIPA 'GOLDEN OXFORD'

Ranunculus asiaticus.
Half-hardy perennial, growing from a tuber. Rich moist soil, full sun. Semi-double & double buttercup-like flowers. *Yellow, orange, red, pink, white.*

Scilla.
Low-growing bulbs. Moist but well-drained soil, sun or part shade. *Pink, excellent blues, white.*

Symphytum COMFREY.
Herbaceous perennials that grow fast & will naturalize freely. Sun or shade. Flowers are bell shaped. *Red, pink, blue, cream, white.*

Tulipa TULIP.
Very large genus of bulbs. Alkaline soil, sun or part shade. *All except blue.*

Viola PANSY & VIOLET.
Low perennials ranging from tiny violets to larger hybrid pansies. Moist but well-drained soil, sun or part shade. *Yellow, gold, orange, red, violet, purple, blue, white.*

🌹 SUMMER 🌹

TREES, SHRUBS, & CLIMBERS

Abutilon.
Half-hardy deciduous shrubs with bell-shaped flowers. Sun with shelter. *Yellow, orange, red, pink, lilac, white.*

Aesculus HORSE CHESTNUT.
Large deciduous trees & shrubs. Sun or part shade. Flowers in panicles. *Pink, white, cream.*

Brugmansia
ANGEL'S TRUMPETS.
Fast-growing tender deciduous & evergreen shrubs (white flowers scented). Sun. Poisonous. *Gold, orange, apricot, pink, purple, white.*

Buddleja.
Fast-growing deciduous shrubs with flowers in panicles. Sun. *Orange, red, pink, purple, lilac, white, cream.*

Ceanothus.
Large evergreen & deciduous shrubs, sometimes small trees. Neutral or acid soil, sun. *Mostly strong blues, some pink & white.*

Cistus ROCK ROSE.
Evergreen shrubs. Sun, shelter. Flowers last one day. *Pink, white.*

Clematis.
Long-flowering, mostly deciduous climbers. Rich soil with roots in shade, shoots in sun. *All except orange, turquoise.*

Cotinus SMOKE TREE.
Large deciduous shrubs or small trees. Sun. *C. coggygria* 'Royal Purple' & others have purple foliage. *Fawn, grey.*

CLEMATIS VENOSA 'VIOLACEA'

CEANOTHUS ARBOREUS 'TREWITHEN BLUE'

Deutzia.
Medium deciduous shrubs. Rich soil, sun. Massed flowers early to midsummer. *Red, pink, white.*

Escallonia.
Tall evergreen shrubs, good for maritime planting. Sun. Flowers resemble spring blossom. *Red, pink, white.*

Eucalyptus GUM TREE.
Fast-growing evergreen trees with attractive foliage. Sun. *E. gunnii, E. pauciflora, E. perriniana* are fairly hardy. *Mostly silver-blue.*

Fremontodendron.
Large evergreen or semi-evergreen shrubs. Light soil, sun with wall shelter. Spring through summer to late autumn. *Yellow.*

Fuchsia.
Mostly tender deciduous shrubs, ideal for containers. Rich soil, part shade. High summer to late autumn. *Orange, red, pink, purple, lilac, white.*

Hebe.
Half-hardy to hardy evergreen shrubs, grown for their flower spikes & foliage. Sun with shelter from cold winds. *Red, pink, purple, blue, white.*

Helianthemum ROCK ROSE.
Small, long-flowering evergreen shrubs. Sun. *Yellow, orange, red, pink, white.*

Heliotropium CHERRY PIE.
Tender evergreen shrubs, usually grown as annuals. Rich soil, sun. Highly scented flowers are borne in corymbs all summer & early autumn. *Violet, purple, white.*

Hibiscus syriacus & its numerous forms.
Long-flowering deciduous shrubs, small trees, & annuals. Sun. Late summer. *Red, pink, purple, white.*

Hypericum ST. JOHN'S WORT.
Deciduous & evergreen shrubs. Sun or part shade. Profuse flowers late summer & autumn. *Yellow.*

Jasminum officinale JASMINE.
Semi-evergreen or deciduous climber. Best in sun. *White.*

Jasminum parkeri, J. revolutum JASMINE.
Evergreen shrubs. Sun. *Yellow.*

Kolkwitzia BEAUTY BUSH.
Large deciduous shrubs. Rich soil, sun. Midsummer. *Pink, white.*

Lantana.
Tender evergreen shrubs, usually grown as annuals, good for containers. Rainbow-coloured flowers. Poisonous. *Yellow, orange, red, pink, white.*

Lavandula LAVENDER.
Hardy & half-hardy mounding evergreen shrubs. Sun. Mid- to late summer. *Pink, purple, lavender, white.*

Lavatera MALLOW.
Short-lived deciduous shrubs & annuals. Sun. *L.* 'Barnsley' is very popular. *Pale pink.*

Lonicera HONEYSUCKLE.
Deciduous & evergreen shrubs & climbers, most with very fragrant flowers. Sun or part shade. (Some sorts flower autumn & winter.) *Yellow, red, pink, cream.*

Olearia DAISY BUSH.
Evergreen shrubs, excellent for maritime planting. Sun with shelter. *O. semidentata* has mauve flowers. *White.*

Passiflora caerulea
PASSION FLOWER.
Frost-hardy, free-flowering evergreen climber. *White flushed pink with purple corona filaments.*

Pelargonium GERANIUM.
Large group of frost-tender sub-shrubs. Sun or bright shade. *Orange, red, pink, purple, white.*

Philadelphus MOCK ORANGE.
Mostly large deciduous shrubs. Sun. *P.* 'Belle Etoile', with white petals blotched purple at base, & *P. microphyllus* & *P.* 'Sybille' (both good for smaller gardens) are favourites. Most *Philadelphus* flowers are highly scented. *White.*

Phlomis JERUSALEM SAGE.
Evergreen shrubs with aromatic grey foliage. Most of the species have whorled flowers. Sun. Slightly tender *P. italica* has lilac-pink flowers. *Mostly yellow.*

Phygelius.
Evergreen or semi-evergreen shrubs & sub-shrubs, usually grown as perennials, with tubular flowers. Sun. Mid- to late summer & autumn. *Yellow, orange, red.*

ROSA 'BIG PURPLE'

Plumbago.
Frost-tender evergreen shrubs, usually grown as annuals, good for containers. Sun. *Sky-blue, white.*

Potentilla.
Long-flowering deciduous shrubs & perennials. Sun or part shade. *P.* 'Manchu' (low with silver foliage) & *P.* 'Vilmoriniana' are recommended. *White, cream.*

Rosa ROSE.
Deciduous shrubs & climbers with variable flowers. Rich moist soil, sun. Through summer & into autumn. *All except blue.*

Santolina.
Aromatic evergreen shrubs. Sun. *S. chamaecyparissus* has silver, *S. pinnata* subsp. *neapolitanum* grey foliage. *Yellow.*

Spartium junceum
SPANISH BROOM.
Deciduous, almost leafless shrub. Light soil, sun. Scented flowers early summer to autumn. *Yellow.*

Weigela.
Medium to large deciduous shrubs. Moist but well-drained soil, sun or part shade. Profuse foxglove-like flowers early to midsummer. *Red, pink, white.*

Wisteria.
Tall deciduous climbers with attractively divided leaves & sweet-scented flowers in long racemes. Sun. *Pink, lilac, white.*

ANNUALS & BIENNIALS

Ageratum.
Low half-hardy annuals with flowers in fluffy corymbs, good for containers. Moist well-drained soil, sun. *Pink, lilac, blue, white.*

Alcea HOLLYHOCK.
Tall perennials best grown as annuals. Rich moist but well-drained soil, sun. Single or double flowers grow up spikes to 3m/15ft. *Yellow, apricot, red, pink, white.*

Antirrhinum SNAPDRAGON.
Perennials best grown as annuals. Sun. Lightly scented flowers. *A. majus* has produced many forms. *Yellow, orange, red, pink, white.*

Arctotis x *hybrida.*
Usually grown as annual. Sun. Bears a succession of large daisy flowers, often zoned. *Yellow, orange, red, pink, white.*

Calceolaria.
Mostly half-hardy annuals & biennials. Rich, moist but well-drained soil, sun. Spotted flowers like tiny inflated balloons. *Yellow, orange, red, pink.*

Calendula POT MARIGOLD.
Self-seeding annuals. Any not too rich soil, sun. Single or double flowers. Dead-head for flowering through summer and autumn. *Yellow, orange, apricot, cream.*

Celosia.
Annuals with cockscombs or plumes of flowers, for planting out early summer or pots. Sun. *Yellow, orange, red, pink, purple, cream.*

Centaurea CORNFLOWER.
Annuals & biennials. Full sun. The wild *C. cyanus* is spectacular blue. *Pink, purple, blues, white.*

Clarkia.
Continuous-flowering annuals, good for cutting. Sun. *Red, pink, salmon, white.*

Coleus.
Evergreen perennials grown as annuals mostly for their foliage. Rich soil, sun. Remove flowers as they appear. *All except blue.*

Convolvulus.
Long-flowering annuals (& perennials). Sun. *Pink, purple, lilac, white.*

Cosmos.
Annuals & perennials with feathery foliage. Light soil, sun. *Yellow, orange, pink, white.*

Digitalis purpurea FOXGLOVE.
Biennial with many forms. Moist well-drained soil, part shade. Tall spikes of spot-throated, hooded flowers early to midsummer. *Rust, pink, purple, white, cream.*

Echium lycopsis.
Bushy, profuse annual. Sun. Mid-summer. *Blue-pink, purple, white.*

Eschscholzia californica.
Long-flowering annual with ferny silver foliage and poppy-like flowers. Sun. *Yellow, orange, red, pink, white.*

Gomphrena
GLOBE AMARANTH.
Annuals with clover-like flowers, good for drying. Full sun. Mid- to late summer. *Yellow, orange, red, pink, purple, white.*

HELICHRYSUM BRACTEATUM

Helichrysum bracteatum
STRAWFLOWER.
Easily grown annual. Sun. *Large range in all except blue, green.*

Iberis umbellata CANDYTUFT.
Low-growing annual. Sun. *Mostly pink, lilac, lavender, some white.*

Lathyrus odoratus SWEET PEA.
Climbing annual with beautifully scented flowers. Rich soil, sun. *Orange, red, pink, violet, purple, blue, white, cream.*

Linaria maroccana
TOADFLAX.
Half-hardy annual with small spurred flowers. Light soil, sun. *Yellow, red, pink, lilac, white.*

Linum FLAX.
Tiny-leaved annuals & perennials with brilliantly coloured flowers. Sun. *Pink, red, yellow, blue.*

Mathiola STOCK.
Annuals & biennials with intensely scented flowers. Sun or part shade. *Red, pink, purple, lilac, white, cream.*

Nemesia.
Profuse, long-flowering annuals. Either neutral or acid soil, sun. Midsummer. *Yellow, orange, red, pink, blue, white.*

Nicotiana TOBACCO PLANT.
Mostly tender perennials usually grown as annuals. Moist, well-drained soil, sun or part shade. *Peach, red, pink, green, white.*

Nigella LOVE-IN-A-MIST.
Annuals easily grown from seed. Sun. Seed pods are decorative in autumn. *Pink, blue, white.*

Petunia.
Free-flowering annuals. Do not plant in the same soil two years running. Sun. Flowers in purple & blue often have good perfume. *Red, pink, violet, purple, blue, white, cream.*

Phacelia campanularia.
Bushy annual. Light soil, sun. *Intense blues.*

Portulaca.
Mostly succulents grown as annuals. Brilliant wide daisy flowers open with the sun. Light soil, full sun. *Yellow, red, pink, purple, white.*

Salvia splendens SAGE.
Very colourful annual with spires of flowers, good for containers. Sun. *Orange, apricot, scarlet, pink, purple, mauve, white.*

Schizanthus.
Tall long-flowering annuals. The flowers often have yellow spotted throats. Rich soil, full sun. *Red, pink, purple, white.*

Silene ROSE OF HEAVEN.
Annuals with bright or pastel flowers. Sun or bright shade. *Pink, lilac, white, cream.*

Tagetes MARIGOLD.
Long-flowering annuals. Sun. Dead-head regularly for best results. *Yellow, gold, orange.*

NICOTIANA 'LIME GREEN'

Tropaeolum majus
NASTURTIUM.
Scrambling annual, also good for containers, with many forms. Sun. Susceptible to aphid attack. *Yellow, orange, red, white, cream.*

Ursinia.
Annuals (& perennials) with finely cut foliage & daisy flowers, ideal for containers. Sun. *Yellow, orange, red.*

Verbena x *hybrida.*
Annual with numerous forms, excellent for containers including hanging baskets. Rich soil, sun. *Red, pink, violet, purple, white.*

Viola x *wittrockiana* PANSY.
Annual. Rich moist well-drained soil, sun or part shade. Numerous forms flower throughout year in mild weather. *All except green.*

Zinnia.
Half-hardy annuals with pompon flowers. Good fertile well-drained soil & plenty of sun. *All (including lime-green) except blue.*

PERENNIALS & BULBS

Aconitum MONKSHOOD.
Perennials with spires of flowers.
Rich moist but well-drained soil,
part shade. All parts poisonous.
Pink, violet, blue, white.

Alchemilla LADY'S MANTLE.
Low perennials spreading rapidly.
Part shade. Flower spires dry well.
Yellow-green.

Allium ORNAMENTAL ONION.
Bulbs. Many sorts have attractive
globular flowerheads. Sun. Late
spring to midsummer. *Yellow,
pink, purple, white.*

AQUILEGIA VULGARIS 'NIVEA'

Alstroemeria.
Perennials with many hybrid
forms. Established plants resent
disturbance. Sun. *Yellow, orange,
red, pink, purple, white.*

Anchusa azurea.
Perennial with flowers in spires to
2m/6ft. Sun. *Intense blues.*

Anigozanthos
KANGAROO PAW.
Half-hardy perennials. Moist acid
soil, sun. *Yellow, mustard, scarlet,
pink, plum, green.*

Aquilegia COLUMBINE.
Medium perennials with spurred
flowers, easily grown from seed.
Moist well-drained soil, sun or
part shade. Early summer. *Yellow,
pink, purple, lilac, blue, white.*

Armeria THRIFT.
Low clump-forming evergreen
perennials with small globes of
flowers, good for maritime
planting. Sun. *Red, pink, white.*

Artemisia LAD'S LOVE,
WORMWOOD.
Perennials, some evergreen or
semi-evergreen, grown for their
aromatic foliage. Sun. Remove
leggy growths & prune to good
shape. *Silver, silver-grey.*

Astilbe.
Moisture-loving perennials with
feathery plumes of flowers. Damp
soil, part shade. Midsummer. *Red,
pink, white.*

Astrantia MASTERWORT.
Medium-sized perennials with
paper-thin flowers. Moist but
well-drained soil, part shade.
Pink, green, white.

Begonia.
Tender perennials mostly from
tubers or rhizomes, usually grown
as annuals, with showy leaves &
profuse flowers. Rich moist well-
drained soil, part shade or shade.
Yellow, orange, red, pink, white.

Borago BORAGE.
Invasive perennials with hairy
leaves & stems of lovely nodding
flowers. Sun or part shade. Low-
growing *B. pygmaea* is particularly
attractive. *Blue, white.*

Campanula BELLFLOWER.
Perennials ranging from rock
plants to taller mid-border sorts.
Sun or part shade. *Pink, purple,
blue, white, cream.*

Canna.
Tall half-hardy perennials with
sword-like leaves sometimes red.
Grow in containers or plant out
early summer, removing indoors
before frost. *Yellow, orange,
scarlet, pink, cream.*

Coreopsis.
Medium-sized perennials (&
annuals) with large daisy flowers.
Light soil, sun. Mid- to late
summer. *Yellow, gold, orange, red.*

Crambe cordifolia KALE.
Perennial with masses of small
flowers held 2m/6ft above very
large leaves. Alkaline soil best,
sun. *White.*

Dahlia.
Perennials growing from tubers
with many flower forms. Plant
late spring, rich soil, sun. Mid-
to late summer. *All except blue,
green.*

Delphinium.
Tall perennials (most need
staking) with flowers in spires.
Rich soil, sun. Cut out flowering
stems when finished for a second
showing. *Pink, purple, excellent
range of blues, white, cream.*

Dianthus PINKS.
Low & taller perennials with
single or double flowers, often
clove scented. Neutral to alkaline
very well-drained soil, sun. Stake
tall sorts. Modern *Dianthus* have
long flowering season. *Yellow,
orange, red, pink, purple, white.*

Erigeron.
Low perennials with profuse daisy
flowers over a long period. Sun.
Pink, violet, purple, lilac.

Eryngium SEA HOLLY.
Medium perennials with silvery
foliage. Flowerheads are thistle-
like & surrounded by decorative
feathery bracts. Sun. *Mostly silver-
blue, some purple, green.*

Euphorbia SPURGE.
Very large genus with many
perennials, grown for their
mounding shape and showy
bracts (*E. griffithii* has red bracts).
Sun. Bracts *Usually lime-green.*

Felicia BLUE MARGUERITE.
Slightly tender perennials often
grown as annuals forming leafy
hummocks. Sun with shelter from
cold winds. Successive flowerings.
Bright blue.

Foeniculum FENNEL.
Decorative tall perennial herb
with feathery foliage and flowers
in umbels. Sun. *Yellow-green.*

DELPHINIUM 'FENELLA'

COREOPSIS GRANDIFLORA
'BADENGOLD'

Filipendula MEADOWSWEET.
Tall perennials with flowers in
panicles. Moist well-drained soil,
sun or part shade. *Pink, white.*

Gaillardia.
Medium perennials (& annuals)
with dazzling daisy flowers. Sun.
Throughout summer & early
autumn. *Yellow, orange, red.*

Galega GOAT'S RUE.
Medium perennials with spires of
pea-like flowers. Sun or part
shade. Needs staking.
Midsummer. *Pink, blue, white.*

Gazania.
Low half-hardy perennials usually
grown as annuals (some have
silver foliage) with large daisy
flowers. Full sun. *Yellow, orange,
red, pink, lime-green, white.*

Geranium CRANESBILL.
Large genus with many low
perennials. Sun or part shade.
*G. cinereum, G. endressii,
G. nodosum, & G. subcaulescens*
are all long flowering. *Carmine,
pink, violet, purple, blue, white.*

Gerbera.
Lowish tender perennials with
rosettes of leaves & showy large
daisy flowers. Sun with shelter.
Yellow, orange, red, pink, white.

Geum.
Small to medium perennials with
rock rose-like flowers. Moist well-
drained soil, sun or part shade.
Orange, red, pink.

Gladiolus.
Medium to tall corms with lily-
like florets opening up tall stems.
Rich soil, sun. *All except blue.*

Gypsophila BABY'S BREATH.
Small to medium perennials with a haze of tiny flowers borne on slender branching stems. Alkaline soil, sun. *Pink, white.*

Hemerocallis DAYLILY.
Medium perennials with lily-like flowers usually borne over a long period. Rich soil, sun or part shade. *Yellow, orange, red, pink, purple, white.*

Impatiens BUSY LIZZIE, BALSAM.
Mostly tender perennials (some annuals), mound-forming, some with decorative leaves. Excellent for containers. Moist well-drained soil, sun, part shade or shade. All need frost protection. *Yellow, orange, red, pink, purple, white.*

Iris.
Growing from a rhizome, plants with sword-like leaves and often sweetly fragrant flowers. Sun. *I. laevigata* & its relatives favour damp places by ponds & streams. Most early summer (some winter or spring). *All colours.*

Kniphofia RED-HOT POKER.
Perennials with tall flower spikes. Many hybrids have silver-green sword-like leaves. Sun. Summer & autumn. *Yellow, orange, red, white, cream.*

Liatris GAYFEATHER.
Medium perennials with strap-shaped leaves. Flowers are borne in spikes. Rich light soil, sun. *Pink, purple, white.*

Lilium LILY.
Large-flowered bulbs usually with several often intensely scented blooms to a stem. Excellent for containers. Rich soil, sun or part shade. *Yellow, orange, red, purple, white, cream.*

Lobelia.
Half-hardy perennials (& annuals). Rich moist well-drained soil, part shade. *L. fulgens* (barely hardy) has scarlet flowers. *Pink, purple, good blues, white.*

Lupinus LUPIN.
Medium to tall perennials with spires of pea-like flowers. Dislikes alkaline soil. Sun or part shade. Prone to aphid attack. Cut back for second flowering. *Yellow, orange, red, pink, purple, blue.*

Lychnis CAMPION.
Small to medium perennials. Sun. *L. coronaria* has silver foliage & strikingly vivid pink flowers. *Orange, red, pink, white.*

Lysimachia LOOSESTRIFE.
Medium-sized perennials that are often invasive. Sun or part shade. *L. nummularia* 'Aurea' is a lovely creeper with flowers & foliage both yellow. *Yellow, white.*

Lythrum PURPLE LOOSESTRIFE.
Medium to tall perennials with flowers in spires. Moist soil, sun or part shade. Midsummer. *Pink.*

PAPAVER NUDICALE
'SUMMER BREEZE'

Meconopsis.
Lovely but short-lived perennials, including wonderful blue poppies *M. betonicifolia* & *M. grandis.* Rich moist but well-drained acid soil, part shade. *Yellow, orange, pink, purple, blue, white.*

Mimulus MONKEY MUSK.
Perennials (annuals & shrubs) with snapdragon-like flowers. Moist soil, sun or part shade. *Yellow, orange, red, pink, white.*

Mirabilis MARVEL OF PERU.
Half-hardy tuberous perennials. Small scented trumpet flowers open in the evening. Rich soil, sun. *Yellow, red, pink, white.*

Monarda didyma BERGAMOT.
Medium-sized perennial (& many forms) with aromatic leaves and whorled flowers. Rich soil, sun. *Red, pink, purple, white.*

Nepeta CATMINT.
Low to medium wide-spreading perennials with spires of flowers over a long period. Sun or part shade. *Lavender, blue, white.*

Nymphaea WATER LILY.
Perennial water plants, many tender, with often scented star-shaped single or double flowers. Rich soil in pool or mesh container, sun or bright shade. *Yellow, red, pink, purple, white.*

Oenothera EVENING PRIMROSE.
Low to tall perennials (& some annuals) with poppy-like flowers. Sun. *Yellow, orange, pink, white.*

Paeonia lactiflora PEONY.
Clump-forming perennial including many hybrids with often scented single or double flowers. Rich moist but well-drained soil, sun or part shade. *Red, pink, cream, white.*

Papaver POPPY.
Medium perennials (& annuals), many self-seeding. Sun. *Yellow, orange, red, pink, purple, white.*

Penstemon.
Low to medium perennials with foxglove-like flowers in spires. Sun. *Red, pink, purple, blue, white.*

Phlox paniculata.
Medium perennial with many forms. Scented flowers are borne in panicles. Rich moist but well-drained soil, sun. *Orange, red, pink, purple, lilac, violet, white.*

Physostegia OBEDIENT PLANT.
Medium perennials with trumpet-shaped flowers in spires. Sun or part shade. *Pink, purple, white.*

Polemonium JACOB'S LADDER.
Medium perennials with ferny foliage. Moist but well-drained soil, sun or part shade. *Blue, lavender, white.*

Polygonum.
Long-flowering perennials (& climbers), sometimes invasive, with flowers in spikes. Moist well-drained soil, sun or part shade. *Red, pink, white.*

Primula.
Perennials with flowers often borne in candelabra form. Moist soil (good by water), sun or part shade. *Yellow, orange, red, pink, purple, white.*

Pyrethrum.
Perennials with daisy flowers. Sun. Early summer. *Red, pink, purple, white.*

Romneya TREE POPPY.
Invasive but beautiful suckering silver-leaved perennials with large sweet-scented poppy flowers. Borderline hardy. Sun. Mid- to late summer. *White.*

Roscoea.
Low to medium tuberous perennials with orchid-like flowers. Rich moist but well-drained soil, part shade. *Yellow, purple, cream, white.*

Scabiosa caucasica SCABIOUS.
Medium perennial with frilled poppy-like flowers. Sun. *Pink, violet, blue, white.*

Sidalcea.
Medium-sized perennials with spires of hollyhock-like flowers borne over a long period. Sun. *Red, pink, white.*

Thalictrum.
Medium to tall perennials with feathery flowers above feathered foliage. Rich moist well-drained soil, sun. *Yellow, pink, lilac, white.*

Tradescantia.
Medium hardy perennials with flowers borne over a long period. Rich moist but well-drained soil, sun or part shade. *Pink, purple, good blues, white.*

Verbascum MULLEIN.
Often tall-stemmed, short-lived perennials (& some annuals). Sun. *V. chaixii* & *V. olympicum* have rosettes of silver leaves. *Yellow, pink, purple, white.*

Veronica SPEEDWELL.
Small to medium perennials with flowers in spikes, often needing support. Rich moist well-drained soil, sun. *Pink, blue, white.*

PRIMULA 'IRIS MAINWARING'

❧ AUTUMN ❧

TREES, SHRUBS, & CLIMBERS

Acer circinatum, A. ginnala, A. japonicum, A. palmatum, A. rubrum & others MAPLE.
Small, medium, & large deciduous trees, many with vivid autumn foliage and some bearing ornamental winged fruits. Moist but well-drained soil, sun or part shade. *Brilliant yellow, gold, orange, red.*

Cotoneaster.
Medium to large deciduous & evergreen shrubs with small white summer flowers followed by coloured berries. Sun. *Yellow, orange, red.*

Erica.
Low evergreen sub-shrubs, many flowering through autumn. Light, moist but well-drained acid soil, sun. *E. cinerea* & *E. vagans* & their forms are recommended. *Pink, purple, white.*

ACER CIRCINATUM

Hydrangea.
Medium to large deciduous shrubs & tall deciduous or evergreen climbers with showy flowerheads. Rich soil (for blue sorts, acid), part shade. Summer to autumn, depending on the form chosen. *Red, pink, purple, blue, white.*

Liriodendron TULIP TREE.
Large deciduous trees grown for their orange & green flowers (produced only on adult plants in summer) and autumn colour. Sun or part shade. *Bright gold.*

Malus coronaria 'Charlottae', **M. trilobata, M. tschonoskii** CRABAPPLE.
Medium deciduous trees with good autumn colour. Rich soil, sun or part shade. *Brilliant gold, red, purple.*

Phygelius.
Half-hardy evergreen shrubs usually grown as hardy perennials. Flowers are trumpet shaped & borne on tall stalks. Sun with shelter. Late summer & autumn. *Yellow, orange, red.*

Pyracantha FIRETHORN.
Large spiny evergreen shrubs with hawthorn-like summer flowers followed by showy berries. Sun or part shade. *Yellow, orange, red.*

Quercus coccinea, Q. rubra, & others OAK.
Stately deciduous trees with fiery foliage. Sun. *Yellow, orange, red.*

ANNUALS & BIENNIALS

Amaranthus caudatus LOVE-LIES-BLEEDING.
Annual with trailing racemes of flowers (*A. hybridus* with upright plumes is also good). Rich soil, sun. *Red, purple, green.*

Callistephus CHINA ASTER.
Low half-hardy annuals with double pompon flowers. Sun. *Yellow, red, pink, purple, white.*

Helianthus annuus SUNFLOWER.
Tall fast-growing large-flowered annual. Sun. Late summer through autumn. *Yellow, gold.*

PERENNIALS & BULBS

Amaryllis BELLADONNA LILY.
Bulbs producing sweet-scented flowers after the leaves. Sun with shelter. *Pink.*

Anemone hupehensis, A. x hybrida.
Small to medium perennials with poppy-like flowers. Rich soil, sun or part shade. Late summer through autumn. *Pink or white.*

CYCLAMEN PSEUDIBERICUM

Aster MICHAELMAS DAISY.
Small to medium perennials with heads of small daisy-like flowers. Rich moist well-drained soil, sun. Susceptible to mildew & wilt but excellent for marvellous displays of colour in autumn. *Rich pinks, purples, violets, blues, white.*

Chrysanthemum.
Large genus of perennials (& some annuals), many flowering in autumn. Forms are variable, from small single daisy-like flowers to very large & showy blooms. Rich soil, sun. *All except blue.*

Cyclamen.
Tuberous perennials, some rarely evergreen. Sun or part shade. (Winter-, spring-, & summer-flowering sorts are also available.) *Carmine, pinks, red-purples, white.*

Dahlia.
Tubers producing small to large single & multi-petalled flowers in a variety of different forms. Best planted late spring. Rich soil, sun. Lift tubers & store frost-free over winter. Late summer through autumn. *All except blue & green.*

Eupatorium HEMP AGRIMONY.
Perennials, often tall growing. Moist but well-drained soil, sun or part shade. Late summer into autumn. *Red, pink, purple, white.*

Gentiana sino-ornata & hybrids GENTIAN.
Low perennials with trumpet flowers, excellent for troughs & pans. All need acid, very well-drained soil, sun. *Intense blues.*

Gladiolus.
Corms with tall flowering stems of lily-like florets that open from the bottom of the stem upward. Rich but very well-drained soil, sun. Lift corms & store frost-free over winter months. Late summer through autumn. *All except blue.*

Helenium.
Medium-sized perennials with sprays of daisy-like flowerheads. Sun. Mid- to late summer and autumn. *Yellow, orange, red.*

Nerine.
Hardy & half-hardy bulbs with stems of trumpet-shaped flowers. Full sun against the shelter of a warm wall. Hardy *N. bowdenii* is particularly good (others need protection from frost). *Orange, red, pink, white.*

Rudbeckia CONEFLOWER.
Medium perennials (annuals & biennials) with daisy-like flowers, excellent for cutting. Sun. *Yellow, orange, red.*

Schizostylis KAFFIR LILY.
Perennials producing spikes of flowers like small gladioli from rhizomes. Borderline hardy. Rich soil, sun with shelter from cold winds. Mid- to late autumn. *Red, pink, white.*

Solidago GOLDENROD.
Mostly large perennials with feathery heads of flowers. Sun or part shade. Although attractive, these are invasive plants that quickly remove nutrients from the soil. *Yellow, gold.*

DAHLIA 'HILLCREST ROYAL'

🌸 WINTER 🌿

TREES, SHRUBS, & CLIMBERS

Aucuba SPOTTED LAUREL.
Medium to large evergreen shrubs including variegated sorts. Plants of both sexes are needed to obtain berry fruits. Part shade or shade. Foliage *Greens or with yellow or cream markings*. Berries *Red*.

Buxus BOX.
Aromatic evergreen shrubs or small trees, ideal for hedging & topiary. Sun or part shade. Main clipping is best done late summer. *Glossy dark green*.

Camellia.
Evergreen shrubs or small trees with glossy green leaves & single or double rose-like flowers (some in spring). Borderline hardy. Rich moist well-drained lime-free soil. *Yellow, red, pink, white*.

Cedrus atlantica f. glauca & others CEDAR.
Evergreen conifers, some with silver-blue needles. Sun. *Silver-blue, greens*.

Chamaecyparis
FALSE CYPRESS.
Evergreen conifers including coloured forms, ranging from miniatures to large trees. Sun. *Greens, gold, blue, silver*.

Chimonanthus WINTERSWEET.
Deciduous wall shrub with waxy, intensely fragrant flowers on bare stems. Rich soil, in the shelter of a sunny wall. *Yellow, cream*.

Cornus alba & forms
DOGWOOD.
Deciduous shrubs with colourful winter shoots, effective beside water. Sun. Shoots *Yellow, red*.

Corylopsis.
Medium to large deciduous shrubs with racemes of sweet-scented flowers. Lime-free soil, sun. Late winter & spring. *Yellow, cream*.

Cryptomeria japonica & forms.
Evergreen conifers grown for their coloured winter foliage. Rich moist but well-drained acid soil, part shade. *Bronze*.

Cupressus CYPRESS.
Small to medium evergreen conifers with tough but feathery foliage in sprays. Sun. *Greens, gold, grey-blue, silver*.

Daphne.
Deciduous & evergreen small to medium shrubs with usually intensely scented flowers. Near neutral soil, sun. Evergreens *D. odora* 'Aureo-marginata', *D. laureola* (no scent, will tolerate shade), & deciduous *D. mezereum* flower winter into spring (other sorts flower spring & summer). *Yellow, pink, green, white*.

SKIMMIA JAPONICA

Hamamelis WITCH HAZEL.
Small deciduous trees. The sweet-scented flowers have delicate spidery petals. Rich moist well-drained lime-free soil, part shade. Late winter. *Yellow, orange, red*.

Hedera IVY.
Medium to tall self-clinging evergreen climbers, some with variegated foliage (*H. helix* 'Tricolor' has a plum-coloured winter flush). Sun or shade. *Green or with gold, cream, or silver marks*.

Ilex HOLLY.
Mostly evergreen shrubs & small to large trees (some variegated) with colourful berry fruits. Rich moist well-drained soil, sun or shade. (Deciduous *I. verticillata* has a profusion of red berries late autumn & early winter). Foliage *Greens & with yellow, white, or cream markings*. Berries *Yellow, orange, red, green, white, black*.

Jasminum nudiflorum
WINTER JASMINE.
Tall hardy deciduous shrub with arching stems. Sun. *Yellow*.

Juniperus JUNIPER.
Small to medium prickly leaved evergreen conifers with coloured forms (in particular low-growing ones). Sun or part shade. *Green, gold, blue, silver*.

Laurus BAY LAUREL.
Medium aromatic evergreen tree, good for large specimen topiaries. Rich soil, sun or part shade with shelter. Plants in pots need occasional waterings in mild winter spells. *Glossy dark green*.

Lonicera HONEYSUCKLE.
See under SUMMER listing.

Mahonia.
Evergreen shrubs with decorative spiky leaves & flowers in racemes. *M.* x 'Charity', *M. japonica*, & *M. lomarifolia* have flowers with scent like lily-of-the-valley. Rich moist but well-drained soil, part shade. *Yellow*.

Picea SPRUCE.
Miniature to large evergreen conifers including forms with coloured foliage (*P. pungens* f. *glauca* is very silvery). Moist well-drained acid soil, sun with shelter. *Green, gold, blue, silver*.

Skimmia.
Medium evergreen shrubs. Plants of both sexes are needed to obtain flowers & berries borne together in winter (but *S. japonica* subsp. *reevesiana* is self fertile). Rich moist but well-drained soil, sun or part shade. Flowers *White opening from pink buds*. Berries *Scarlet*.

Taxus baccata YEW.
Medium evergreen conifer, excellent for topiary & hedges, females with red fruit ('Lutea' has yellow). Sun or shade. *Dark green*.

Viburnum.
Small to large deciduous & evergreen shrubs. Rich moist but well-drained soil, sun. Deciduous *V.* x *bodnantense* (vanilla scented) & *V. farreri* flower on bare stems. Evergreen *V. tinus* flowers autumn to spring. *Pink, white*.

PERENNIALS & BULBS

Bergenia.
Low evergreen perennials with large rounded leaves. Sun or part shade. Flowers are produced in mild winter weather & through spring. *Pink, purple, white*.

Crocus.
Low bulbs, best grown in large swaths. Sun. Mid- to late winter, depending on weather (some sorts flower in autumn). *Yellow, orange, red, pink, purple, blue, white*.

Eranthis WINTER ACONITE.
Low tuber bearing buttercup-like flowers surrounded by rosettes of leaves. Moist but well-drained soil, sun. Midwinter. *Yellow*.

Galanthus SNOWDROP.
Bulbs with delicate bell-shaped flowers. Moist but well-drained soil, part shade. Depending on weather, midwinter to spring. *White with green markings*.

Helleborus CHRISTMAS ROSE, LENTEN ROSE.
Evergreen & semi-evergreen perennials. Rich moist but well-drained soil, part shade. *H. niger* from early winter; *H. orientalis* 'Atrorubens' & *H. viridis* mid- & late winter & early spring. *Pink, green, white, cream*.

Iris.
See under SUMMER listing.

GALANTHUS FOSTERI

INDEX

Page numbers that appear in **bold type** refer you to a plant featured in a "Related Colour Swatch". Page numbers that appear in normal roman type direct you to text on a plant or subject. Page numbers that appear in *italic type* direct you to a picture with a caption.

GARDEN CREDITS

Publisher's Note to Readers

Many of the gardens that were photographed by Steven Wooster for *Malcolm Hillier's Colour Garden* will be found on this page; but where people have asked not to be included, their desire for anonymity has been respected and their names and the locations of their gardens do not appear. The publisher would be grateful to be told of unintended errors, omissions, or incorrectly named plants. In the credits, a letter following a page number shows picture position: t = top; b = bottom; c = centre; l = left; r = right. No letter identifies a full-page picture.

- **Ayrlies Garden** (New Zealand), Bev & Malcolm McConnell 73t, 79t
- **Barnsley House,** Rosemary Verey 28bl, 112t
- **Bates Green Farmhouse,** Mr. & Mrs. J. McCulthan 102b
- **Kathy Boardman & Serena Blackie** (New Zealand) 71b
- **Bodnant Garden** 46b, 57t
- **Bourton House Garden,** Mr. & Mrs. R. Paice 86b
- **Brook Cottage,** Mr. & Mrs. D. Hodges 22t, 45t
- **The Winter Garden at The Cambridge Botanic Gardens** 34r, 132 & 133, 136b, 138b
- **The Beth Chatto Gardens** 22b, 32t, 32b, 35t, 35b, 43tr, 49b, 50bl, 53t, 60 & 61, 73b, 85t, 95t, 97t, 97b, 122b, 129t
- **Mrs. Chea** 92t
- **Chiffchaffs,** Mr. & Mrs. K.R. Potts 48bl, 59t
- **Mrs. Cooke** (New Zealand) 85bl
- **Denmans Garden,** John Brookes 31t, 31br, 46t, 68t, 115t
- **East Lambrook Manor,** Mr. & Mrs. A. Norton 52t, 81t, 119
- **Elizabeth & Roger Edmonds** (New Zealand) 74b
- **Feeringbury Manor,** Mr. & Mrs. Giles Coode Adams 42t
- **Fitz House,** Major Mordaunt-Hare 67, 84
- **Fulham Park Gardens,** Anthony Noel 92b
- **Gardens of the Mind,** Ivan Hicks 64t, 69t

- **Gethsemane Garden** (New Zealand), Bev & Ken Loader 72t, 108b
- **Great Dixter,** Christopher Lloyd 12b, 31bl, 56t, 65t, 66b, 76bl, 77, 78b, 85br, 94b, 99t, 99b, 100b, 104b,111t, 116t, 118t, 125t, 125b, 126t, 127t, 131t
- **Hadspen House,** Nori & Sandra Pope 10b, 78t, 104t, 105b
- **Hampton Court Gardens** 47tr, 50br, 51
- **Hazelby House,** Prue & Martin Lane-Fox 28t, 111b
- **The Sir Harold Hillier Gardens & Arboretum** 128
- **Isabella Plantation,** Richmond Park 48t, 55t, 56b
- **Kelberdale,** Stan & Chris Abbot 89b
- **Kennerton Priory,** The Hon. Mrs. Healing 24b, 33t, 33b, 76br
- **The Keukenhof Gardens** (Holland) 14b, 24c, 44b, 59b
- **Leonardslee Garden,** The Loder Family 58
- **Elizabeth Luisetti** (New Zealand) 116b, 118b
- **Luquis** (New Zealand) 81b
- **Matai Moana,** Daphne & Hugh Wilson 37t, 80, 87t, 107t
- **The Mien Rhys Gardens** (Holland) 68b, 71t, 103t
- **Milton Lodge,** Mr. D.C. Tudway Quilter 87t
- **Nymans Garden** 108b
- **Ohinetahi** (New Zealand), John & Pauline Trengrove 93, 105t, 112b
- **Owl Cottage** Mrs. A.L. Hutchinson 72b

- **Putsborough Manor,** Mr. & Mrs. T.W. Bigge 76t
- **Saling Hall,** Hugh & Judy Johnson 16b, 40b, 42b
- **St. Paul's Walden Bury** Simon Bowes Lyon 18b
- **Sticky Wicket,** Peter & Pam Lewis 88, 89t
- **Kitty & Victor Sunde** (New Zealand) 106b, 109
- **Titoki Point** (New Zealand), Gordon & Annette Collier 66t, 82t, 90b, 114, 115b, 117t
- **Turn Ends** 38 & 39
- **Waimarino** (New Zealand), Liz & Rod Morrow 75t
- **Westonbirt Arboretum** 120 & 121
- **White Windows,** Mr. & Mrs. B. Sterndale Bonnett 91t
- **Wilsons Mill** (New Zealand), Mr. & Mrs. Izard 101t, 159
- **Winterhome Garden** (New Zealand), Susan & Richard McFarlane 83t

ACKNOWLEDGMENTS

Author's Acknowledgments

Firstly, and most importantly, I would like to thank my business partner Quentin Roake, who has shared, advised, and encouraged throughout the production of *Colour Garden* with his keen intelligence and critical objectivity.

Special thanks also to the two photographers, Steven Wooster, who has captured in all the outdoor location pictures (including those in the section on colour theory) the colours and moods of the seasons with such inspired clarity; and Stephen Hayward, whose studio shots for the section on colour theory, as well as the seasonal plant palettes and plant colour swatches, form a stunning addition to the book.

Finally, I would like to thank friends at the Richmond Office of Dorling Kindersley, in particular project editor Gillian Roberts and art editor Debbie Myatt, who are together so inspirational a team, and who help to make all our work into such a happy experience.

Publisher's Acknowledgments

Thanks to Hilary Bird for the index; Mark Bracey for computer support; Christopher Brickell for identifying *Reseda lutea* and *Lysimachia vulgaris*; Caroline Church for the line artworks; Elaine Hewson for design help; Isobel Holland & Bella Pringle for editorial help; Mel Roberts for being a devoted & exacting editorial guardian angel.

The Commissioned Photographs

Studio photographs and the location picture on page 140 *(bottom right)* by Stephen Hayward. Outdoor location pictures by Steven Wooster. Plant portraits for Seasonal Plant Ideas as follows: Andy Butler (146 *left*, 148 *top*, 150 *right*); Clive Boursnell (148 *left*, *right*); Eric Crichton (151 *right*); Howard Rice (152 *left*); Neil Fletcher (147 *centre* & *right*, 149 *right*, 151 *centre*, 152 *right*); Andrew Lawson (147 *left*, 150 *left*); Steven Wooster (146 *right*, 149 *left*, 150 *centre*, 152 *centre*, 153 *left* & *right*).

OTHER PICTURE CAPTIONS

Outdoor location pictures on pages 1 & 4 are described in "Random Planting" (p. 73) & "Daring Display" (p. 108). Those on pages 2, 5, 159, & 160 are described below.

ENTICING PATHWAY

Bosky shade welcomes the wanderer and beckons on into the cool darkness of woods. Filtering through, sun sheds playful summer light over pink, yellow, and a host of lowly greens.

ZESTFUL CONTRAST

Against lime-green euphorbia bracts, a single glorious pink tulip looks almost edible. Sharp greens in foliage or flowers give a boost to almost every other colour in the garden.

HAPPY DAYS

A tumult of gentle country hues leads lupins, catmint, roses, Jerusalem sage, and foxgloves into a joyful disarray of purples and pinks, highlighted by primrose-yellow and white.

SUNNY SIDE OF THE HEDGE

An ancient wild pear stands gaunt, looming over the bastion of a great yew hedge. Its grey bark is warmed and soothed by shafts of brilliant autumn sun and the azure sky.